MW00568741

# CRIME
## in Canada

# CRIME
## in Canada

DIANE CROCKER

ISSUES IN CANADA

OXFORD
UNIVERSITY PRESS

AURORA PUBLIC LIBRARY

# OXFORD
UNIVERSITY PRESS

Oxford University Press is a department of the University of Oxford.
It furthers the University's objective of excellence in research, scholarship,
and education by publishing worldwide. Oxford is a registered trade mark of
Oxford University Press in the UK and in certain other countries.

Published in Canada by
Oxford University Press
8 Sampson Mews, Suite 204,
Don Mills, Ontario M3C 0H5 Canada

www.oupcanada.com

Copyright © Diane Crocker 2012

The moral rights of the author have been asserted

Database right Oxford University Press (maker)

All rights reserved. No part of this publication may be reproduced,
stored ina retrieval system, or transmitted, in any form or by any
means, without theprior permission in writing of
Oxford University Press, or as expressly permitted
by law, by licence, or under terms agreed with the appropriate
reprographics rights organization. Enquiries concerning
reproduction outside the scope of the above should be sent to the
Permissions Department at the address above or through the following
url:  www.oupcanada.com/permission/permission_request.php

Every effort has been made to determine and contact copyright holders.
In the case of any omissions,the publisher will be pleased to make suitable acknowledgement in
future editions.

**Library and Archives Canada Cataloguing in Publication**

Crocker, Diane
Crime in Canada / Diane Crocker.
(Issues in Canada)

Includes bibliographical references and index.
ISBN 978-0-19-543247-3

1. Criminal justice, Administration of—Canada.  2. Crime—Canada.

3. Crime—Canada—Public opinion. 4. Canada—Public opinion.
I. Title. II. Series Issues in Canada.

HV9960.C2C76 2010     364.971        C2009-907444-3

Cover image: © iStockphoto.com/kenb

Printed and bound in the United States of America.

1 2 3 4 — 15 14 13 12

# Contents

# List of Figures

# Acknowledgements

Along the way, many people helped me write this book. I would like to first thank Lorne Tepperman for his invitation to write the book and unwavering interest along the way. Jennie Rubio and Katie Scott provided outstanding editorial support. Several colleagues read sections and pointed me to relevant resources. I should thank Kevin Bonnycastle, Rebecca Kong, Dawn Moore, Stephen Schneider, John Turner, and Russell Westhaver in this regard. Research assistance was provided by Amanda Nelund who left no stone unturned in tracking down sources. I owe a great deal to Ron Crocker, whose curiosity and interest helped hone many of my underdeveloped ideas on topics discussed throughout this book. Thanks too to my family for letting me work late into the night.

Acknowledgements

# Abbreviations

CAMH  Centre for Addiction and Mental Health

CCRA  Corrections and Conditional Release Act

COSA  Circles of Support and Accountability

CPTSD Crime Prevention Through Social Development

CSC  Correctional Service of Canada

GSS  General Social Survey

NCPC  National Crime Prevention Centre

PRCSI  Police-Reported Crime Severity Index

UCR  Uniform Crime Reporting Survey

# CRIME
## in Canada

# The Crime Problem in Canada

*We've been hearing across the country that crime rates are going down, but it just feels in talking to ordinary Canadians that they don't feel as safe as they felt 20 years ago, so that would seem to contradict some of the statistical information that we in fact are privy to.*

Charles Momy,
Canadian Police Association President[1]

*We keep hearing that crime is going down but I am not so sure that is true.*

Myron Thomson,
Canadian MP representing Wild Rose, Alberta[2]

## Statistics

Despite the reservations raised in the quotes above, the rate of crime in Canada has been decreasing. Even so, crime remains a key topic of media interest. While media stories do occasionally acknowledge the drop in crime, they are also usually quick to note specific areas in which crime is increasing. A 2009 Vancouver *Province* headline declared, "The homicide rate stays flat, despite rise in gang shootings." Politicians and other public figures also tend to provide mixed messages, suggesting that despite the drop in crime, we are in the grips of a crime wave. Some commentators argue that Canadians' level of fear or concern about crime is in and of itself adequate proof of a problem.

The media also report disproportionately on violent crime. One study in Ottawa found that more than half of the stories in the local news involved a violent crime, when in reality only 7 percent of crime in Ottawa is violent (Gabor 1994)—recalling the old media adage that "if it bleeds it leads." What can we say about the true picture of crime in Canada?

Crime is measured in two ways: police data and victimization surveys. Statistics Canada uses police data from the Uniform Crime Reporting Survey (UCR) to compile an annual crime rate and a crime severity index. Every five years, Statistics Canada includes questions on victimization in the General Social Survey (GSS) to produce victimization rates. Police data tell us only about crimes that are reported to the police, whereas the data from victimization surveys shed light on crimes that do not come to the attention of the police. The annual reporting of the crime rate typically attracts widespread media coverage.

In 2009 Canada's violent crime rate was 1,314 incidents reported to the police for every 100,000 adults in Canada. The property crime rate was 4,081 per 100,000 people. Violent crime made up only 20 percent of crimes reported to the police. As in other years almost half of violent crime was "common assault," the least serious type of assault.[3] More serious assaults were far less frequent. Assaults with a weapon and assaults causing bodily harm accounted for 12 percent of violent crime reported in 2009 and made up less than 3 percent of all crime in Canada. Property crimes are much more prevalent, but the bulk of these incidents are also the less serious types. In 2009 mischief and theft under $5,000 made up just over half the property crimes reported to the police (Dauvergne and Turner 2010).

Although Canada did see increases in the crime rate in the 1970s and 1980s, the amount of police-reported crime has been decreasing in recent decades. In 2008 the crime rate reached a 30-year low. We have seen some fluctuations in the rate of violent crime, which generally increased between 1998 and 2000 but has been declining slightly since then. Serious assaults were among the few types of violent crime that have increased in recent years. The homicide rate also went up in 2008, as a result of an increase in the number of gang-related homicides (Beattie 2009; Gannon et al. 2005; Wallace 2009). The number of homicides in Canada is still below the peak rate of the 1970s (Dauvergne and Turner 2010).

The example of homicide reveals one major limitation to depending on crime rates for providing an accurate overall picture. There are approximately 600 homicides in Canada every year, compared with more than 500,000 incidents of theft under $5,000. Most people would agree that homicide is the more serious crime, but the crime rate counts each homicide as one incident and each theft as one incident. This means that the crime rate is dominated by crimes that happen relatively often but are among the least serious. Small changes in the number of serious crimes

# Crime Waves?

Jeffrey Rosenthal is a professor of statistics at the University of Toronto who describes the situation in Toronto in 2003:

> In the first week of November 2003, five separate homicides were recorded in the Greater Toronto metropolitan region, an area that averages just 1.5 homicides per week. This fact was widely reported in the media, amid fears of a huge and increasing crime wave. Toronto's police chief called for a public inquiry into the judicial system, saying it "provides no apparent deterrent." Was such a concern justified? (Rosenthal 2005, 17–18)

He explains this apparent crime wave as a statistical phenomenon, not a crime problem. According to his calculations, it is possible for Toronto to have five homicides a week once every 71 weeks or almost once a year. This is possible because some events will randomly clump together with no particular reason. "By contrast," he continues, "each week has just over 22 % probability of being completely homicide-free, and indeed Toronto experiences many weeks without any homicides at all. But I have yet to see a newspaper headline that screams 'No Murders This Week!'" (Rosenthal 2005, 19)

(such as homicide) will have little effect on the overall crime rate because they are relatively infrequent. Likewise, an increase in the number of incidents of mischief will drive the crime rate up. Because the crime rate relies on counting the number of crime incidents that are reported to the police, it essentially measures volume of crime. As such, it can easily hide small but potentially worrying increases in serious crimes (Wallace et al. 2009).

To address these limitations, Statistics Canada recently developed a Police-Reported Crime Severity Index (PRCSI) to supplement the crime rate. The PRCSI counts police-reported crime and weighs each incident based on seriousness. Instead of one murder and one theft counting as two equal crimes, murder is weighed more heavily. The weight for a given crime is based on the sentences given out by the courts and the incarceration rate. Crimes that are punished more severely—with harsher sentences and higher rates of incarceration—have more weight in the index. For example, the weight for murder is 9.125, whereas the weight for cannabis possession is only 7. The index therefore takes into account not only changes in crime volume, but also changes in the seriousness of crimes. The PRCSI, then, reveals a more nuanced picture of crime in Canada and facilitates comparisons across regions (Wallace et al. 2009).

# Crime in Canada and the United States

Some argue that our perception of crime in Canada is driven by images of crime in the US. Comparing crime rates is complicated by the fact that our legal definitions vary. Statistics Canada has accounted for these issues and finds that the overall crime rate in the US is much higher than in Canada. The US homicide rate is three times higher. Figure 1-1 shows that the rate of violent crime in the US is double that in Canada, with twice the rate of aggravated assault and robbery. Property crime rates are similar, although Canada has a higher rate of motor vehicle theft and break and enter (Canadian Centre for Justice Statistics 2001).

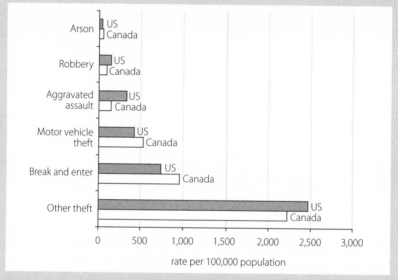

**Figure 1-1  Crime Rate by Type of Crime, Canada and US**
Source: Adapted from Canadian Centre for Justice Statistics 2001

Despite the differences in rates of crime, patterns over time are fairly similar in both countries. Crime in the United States, like in Canada, began to decrease in the mid-1990s and has been declining ever since (Canadian Centre for Justice Statistics 2001).

The PRCSI shows an astonishing 21 percent decrease in overall crime severity across Canada between 1998 and 2007. This decrease is more than the decrease seen in the crime rate, meaning that the severity of crime decreased more than the volume of police-reported crime. The severity of violent crime has remained fairly stable over time (Wallace et al. 2009).

Measures of crime drawn from police data are limited because they count only those crimes that have been reported to the police; clearly, not all crimes are reported. In fact, the crime rate and the PRCSI tell us more about the work being done by police than about the actual amount of crime in our communities. The GSS is our source of victimization data in Canada. Run every five years, it is a poll of approximately 24,000 Canadians that asks questions about eight different types of crime. It also asks those who identify themselves as having been victims of crime for details about their experiences: How were they affected by the crime? Did they report the crime? Who did they turn to for support? Did they use any of the services available for victims of crime? The GSS shows that only about one-third of crimes come to the attention of the police, and also that some crimes are less likely to be reported than others. For example, sexual assaults are the least reported crime with fewer than 10 percent of incidents being reported to police. This crime is deeply personal and often carries a stigma, making victims less likely to report it. Other crimes do not carry a stigma. For example, about half of robberies, break and enters, and motor vehicle thefts are reported to police (Aucoin and Beauchamp 2007; Gannon and Mihorean 2005; Perreault and Brennan 2010). Indeed, the reporting of these crimes is encouraged because of rules associated with insurance policies.

According to the GSS completed in 2009, about one-quarter of Canadian adults had been victimized by at least one crime in the previous year. This statistic is not significantly different from that found in the 2004 and 1999 surveys. Violent victimization rates have remained stable, but the rate of personal property theft has increased (Perreault and Brennan 2010). Men and women have similar rates of violent victimization. Men have higher rates of physical assault and robbery whereas women have higher rates of sexual assault. The risk of violent victimization is highest among young people (15 to 24 years old), and Aboriginal Canadians are twice as likely as non-Aboriginal peoples to report having been victimized (Perreault and Brennan 2010). Compared internationally, our victimization rate is about average (Sauvé and Hung 2008).

## Public Knowledge of Crime

The statistics demonstrate that police-reported crime is decreasing and that the severity of the crimes reported is also decreasing. Victimization rates are stable and in line with international rates. Public opinion, however, suggests that Canadians do not believe this to be the case. By and large, the general public in Canada believes that crime is increasing. A poll in 1990 found that 72 percent of Canadians believed that crime was going up (Adams 1990). A recent Angus Reid poll found that just under half of Canadians believe that the crime rate is on the rise; only

# Crime in the North

The crime rate in the northern territories is substantially higher than rates reported in the southern provinces. Nunavut and the Northwest Territories have crime rates that are more than five times higher than the overall rate in Canada. The police-reported crime rate in the Yukon is three times higher than the national rate and almost double the rate of the province with the next highest, Manitoba.

The PRCSI reveals something more about the nature of crime in northern communities relative to crime in the south. While the crime severity index for the territories is still higher than it is for the provinces, the difference between the crime severity index in the north and south is smaller than the difference between the crime rates.

one-quarter are aware that it is actually going down (Makin 2010). While recent data are scant, an earlier survey found that Canadians dramatically overestimated the number of violent crimes that occurred relative to other crimes (Doob and Roberts 1983). Few Canadians know that the severity of crime in our country is decreasing (Makin 2010). This disconnect between public opinion and the data is cause for concern, given that misinformation about crime can lead the public to push for misplaced and unnecessary solutions.

Perhaps an even greater problem lies in the public's lack of confidence in the criminal justice system. The National Justice Survey found that Canadians express higher levels of confidence in many other major public institutions, such as health and education, than they do in the criminal justice system. Looking at different sectors of the justice system, Canadians express the highest level of confidence in the police and the lowest level of confidence in the youth justice and parole systems (Latimer and Desjardins 2007). This lack of confidence is another cause for concern; for justice to be done properly, people must have faith in the system that administers it: in the words of a prominent criminologist, "Power can be assigned, but legitimacy and authority have to be earned" (Roberts 2004a).

We saw above that fear of crime often enters the political arena. Some politicians routinely argue that, even if crime is going down, justice must be robust—we must be tough on crime—in order to reassure people. However, surveys do not conclusively demonstrate that Canadians are terribly fearful. In the 2004 General Social Survey, most of those polled reported feeling fairly safe when walking alone or taking public transportation. The level of satisfaction with the criminal justice system has been increasing, and the level of worry about personal safety has been decreasing (Gannon 2004). This, however, rarely gets reported.

## Canadians' Views on Solutions

Added to the lack of confidence is a public concern about inadequate sentencing. One survey found that 74 percent of Canadians believed that sentences are too lenient (Roberts, Crutcher, and Verbrugge 2007). In another, one-third of Ontarians felt that harsher sentences would be the best way to control crime committed by adults (Doob 2000). Research has also found that mandatory minimum sentences—considered a fairly harsh option because they limit the discretion individual judges may employ—were supported by slightly more than half of respondents (Roberts, Crutcher, and Verbrugge 2007). When asked about mandatory minimum sentences for serious drug crimes, almost all Canadians polled in a recent survey supported this option (Angus Reid 2009b).

At first blush, these surveys suggest that Canadians take a punitive approach to crime. But a closer look reveals a more nuanced picture. The 1999 General Social Survey presented a sample of Canadians with hypothetical crime scenarios. People were asked to suggest a sentence for the offender. More people chose a prison sentence for adults than for young offenders. They were also more likely to want prison sentences for repeat offenders. The type of crime further affected their choice of punishment for adults. Canadians were more likely to choose prison for break and enter than for minor assault. The survey asked a follow-up question to people who preferred prison for the various scenarios: Would it be acceptable for a judge to sentence the offender to probation and community service? At least one-third of those who initially supported a prison sentence accepted the alternative, suggesting some ambivalence about their initial choice of prison (Tufts 2000; Tufts and Roberts 2002).

Generally, the sentences recommended by the general public were similar to the types of sentences given by the courts in real cases. This suggests that in reality the public is not necessarily more punitive than the judiciary; it suggests that public response may reflect a lack of knowledge about the reality of sentencing. It may be that Canadians hear only about anomalous cases that attract media attention because the sentences seem light. They do not hear about the many thousands of typical sentences handed out every day in Canadian courts.

Canadians are also fairly open to prison alternatives. One survey found that 65 percent of people polled in Ontario preferred the use of such alternatives and that only 35 percent preferred more prisons

## Public Punitiveness in International Perspective

Countries all over the world participate in the International Criminal Victimization Survey. Across all the countries surveyed in 2004–5, 33 percent of respondents opted for imprisonment for a burglar who had committed other crimes in the past. Looking only at the Canadian respondents it appears that Canadian attitudes are more punitive; 44 percent opted for a prison sentence. A similar proportion of Americans (47 percent) shared this view. This contrasts with less than 15 percent in Austria, France, and Switzerland. The most punitive country was Mexico, with 70 percent of respondents opting for imprisonment when given the same scenario (van Dijk, van Kesteren, and Smit 2007).

for adults (Doob 2000). The General Social Survey also found a high level of support for the use of community-based sentences for first-time offenders. It asked victims about their support for victim-offender mediation programs, which typically involve a face-to-face meeting facilitated by a trained mediator who works with the victim and offender to find a suitable way to deal with the crime. The GSS also found that just over half of victims of property or household crime were supportive of mediation. About one-third of victims of violent crime said that they might pursue mediation if it was available (Tufts 2000). Another survey found that support for conditional sentences (for example, house arrest) varied depending on the crime, but that many members of the public were willing to use conditional sentences for more than just property crime (Sanders and Roberts 2000). These research findings speak to the complexity of public opinion; it cannot simply be characterized as punitive.

The proportion of probationary and custodial sentences has not changed much since 2002.[4] We have, however, seen an overall decrease in the length of custodial sentences. Despite this overall trend, some crimes are generating longer jail terms: attempted murder, robbery, criminal harassment, and drug trafficking. The average length of probation—one year—has been stable since Statistics Canada started collecting this data in the mid-1990s. Terms of probation have gone up for attempted murder, drug possession, and sexual assault but down for criminal harassment (i.e., stalking) (Marth 2008). It appears then that judges are using more prison terms and less probation for offenders charged with stalking. They have increased punishment for both trafficking and possessing drugs, with a focus on increasing prison terms for traffickers.

# Past Responses to Crime

Prison and probation are the most widely used sentences for crime in Canada. Because judges sometimes give an offender more than one sentence—for example prison and probation—sentences can be counted in two ways. We can count either the total number of sentences given or only the most serious sentence if more than one has been given. In an evaluation of all the sentences handed out in Canadian courts, we find that probation is used in just under half the cases sentenced in Adult Criminal Court. In many instances, however, probation is used in conjunction with another punishment. Figure 1-2 shows that probation is the most serious sentence in almost one-third of cases. Prison is the most serious sentence in just over one-third of cases; fines are the most serious in just over one-quarter (Marth 2008).

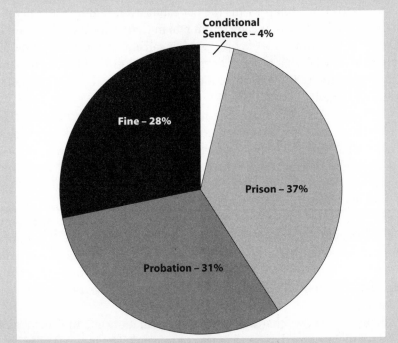

**Figure 1-2  Distribution of Sentences in Canadian Courts**
Source: Adapted from Canadian Centre for Justice Statistics 2008

It would be easy to assume that crimes against the person are more likely to result in a custodial sentence than crimes against property. This is not, however, the case. Just under 33 percent of cases involving a crime against the person (e.g., assaults, threats) resulted in a prison sentence, while 40 percent of offenders found guilty of crimes against property were given a term of imprisonment. It therefore appears as if we sentence more harshly in cases of property crime than in cases of personal crime; however, a closer examination of the data shows that if common assault—the least serious form of assault—is not included, then the incarceration rate for crimes against the person is 44 percent, higher than the incarceration rate for property crime. Furthermore, the average prison term for a violent offence is 70 days, compared to just over 40 days for crimes against property. It may also be useful to note that offenders found guilty of crimes against property tend to have longer criminal histories, which in turn tend to lead to harsher sentences (Marth 2008). Looking at the bigger picture shows that our courts direct more punitive sentences to those convicted of violent offences.

The incarceration rate is often used as an indicator of how a country responds to crime. It represents the per capita average number of people in prison each day. The incarceration rate in Canada peaked in the mid-1990s. At that time, 150 people were incarcerated for every 100,000 adults in Canada. That number decreased until 2005 but has been rising again since. In 2009 the incarceration rate was 138 people per 100,000 adults in Canada.[5]

As Figure 1-3 shows, Canada has among the highest incarceration rates relative to many European countries. But the United States, as a result of harsh mandatory sentences and other crime-control policies, has the highest incarceration rate by far (International Centre for Prison Studies 2010).

The increasing incarceration rate in Canada does not, however, mean that more people are being sentenced to serve time in prison. The incarceration rate is a crude count of people held in jail. It does not account for key distinctions in the reasons for incarceration. An individual can be in jail for a number of reasons: while on remand, awaiting trial of sentencing, or after being formally sentenced to a period of incarceration.

Figure 1-4 shows that the growing incarceration rate in Canada is a result of the increased use and length of remand. The number of people in remand now surpasses the number of people serving a custodial sentence. Some consider these numbers to represent a major crisis in the correctional system that has led to overcrowding and a deterioration of conditions in pre-trial or pre-sentence detention facilities. Even provincial governments across the country have complained that the remand population is making it difficult for them to properly operate provincial jails (Galloway 2011).

Many criminologists and others working in the system have speculated about the rise in the remand population. It could be related to increases in court processing time or changes in laws governing

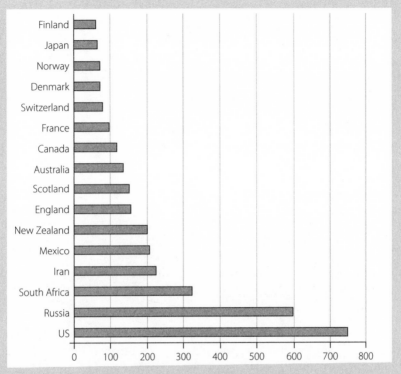

**Figure 1-3  International Incarceration Rates, 2010**
Source: Adapted from International Centre for Prison Studies 2010

sentencing and bail (Johnson 2003; Landry and Sinha 2008). Data also suggest that remand numbers are increasing due to the growing number of charges for crimes against the administration of justice (Taillon 2006). These charges include failure to appear in court or comply with conditions imposed by the court, and often result in a judge imposing remand to ensure compliance. Lack of bail supervision programs may also be contributing to the increasing number of accused for whom judges deny bail. Saskatchewan has such a program and is the only province to have had a decrease in remand numbers. Judges in that province may be more comfortable releasing people on bail, knowing that they will still be supervised.

In the past, time served in remand has been credited at the time of sentencing. In some cases, offenders received a two-for-one credit for time served in pre-sentence detention. This meant that a person who waited in remand for three months, for example, and was subsequently sentenced to a one-year jail term could have had up to six months

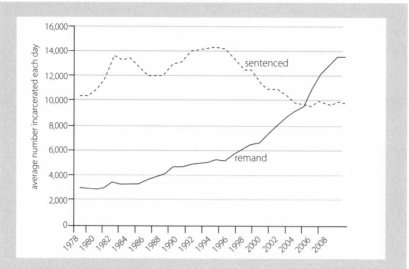

**Figure 1-4  Incarceration Rate Growth with Use of Remand**
Source: Adapted from Statistics Canada n.d.

credited to his or her final sentence and deducted from the one-year sentence. Some suggest that this policy created a motive for defence lawyers to delay court processes (White 2010). Defence lawyers, according to this argument, stalled in order to have their clients spend more time on remand, and therefore less time serving their sentences.

No research has confirmed whether this practice was widespread or what other factors have contributed to the increase in the remand population. The trend is worrying for several reasons. First, those who cannot afford to pay bail are disproportionately serving time in remand. Second, the conditions in many remand centres are generally quite poor. Few centres have the programs or services that are available in provincial jails or federal prisons. Third, incarcerating an individual who has not been found guilty, or who is waiting for a sentence that could be shorter than the time spent waiting, may be inherently unjust. Time spent in remand also does not count toward parole eligibility. The Supreme Court of Canada has upheld the practice of giving double credit for time waiting in remand, arguing that it makes up for the problems associated with time spent in remand.

## The Way Forward

The Truth in Sentencing Act, passed in February 2010, changed the longstanding practice of double credit for time served.  The new law restricts the ability of judges to apply a credit for pre-sentencing or pre-trial remand. When tabling the bill, the justice minister argued that "there are many people across Canada, myself included, who would like to see more truth in sentencing, in the sense that the sentence you get is the sentence you serve" (Mayeda 2009). Advocates of the bill also expect the new law will eliminate the stalling tactics that they believe are clogging up the system (White 2010). Opponents of the bill argue that people held in remand are typically those who are unable to post bail and that the bill will thus disproportionately affect the mentally ill, Aboriginal offenders, and others who lack the means to secure bail. Furthermore, these opponents argue that judges already have the power to deny credit if they suspect a lawyer is stalling or if they believe the conditions in remand were quite good.

Others contend that as a result of the bill, offenders will spend more time in prison, costing more money yet providing no improvement in public safety. The Parliamentary Budget Officer estimates that it will cost one billion dollars annually to implement the change (Rajekar and Mathilakath 2010). Time will tell whether the bill has its intended consequences; in the meantime, it is clear that the bill will increase the incarceration rate in Canada while costing a great deal of money. It will also not decrease the remand population. In effect, those in the system will have to spend more time incarcerated than what their sentence dictates. This may not be the kind of "truth" in sentencing that Canadians want to achieve.

Certainly, Canadians have much to consider about what kind of legislative change will have a real effect on public safety. The government recently brought back 37 pieces of proposed legislation that died at the time of prorogation in 2010. One-third of them relate to crime and many will be expensive (Piché 2010). If passed, Bill C-16 will amend the Criminal Code so that fewer offenders will be able to serve their sentences in the community. Bill S-6 proposes to repeal the "faint hope clause" that allows offenders serving a life sentence to apply for accelerated parole. Bill C-39 lays out changes to the Correctional and Conditional Release Act that will tighten up parole eligibility rules.[6] Our current government is working under the assumption that legislative changes that promote custodial sentences are an appropriate response to crime in Canada.

The current political climate is shifting our response to crime toward a more American model in which incarceration and punishment are key tools. Traditionally, Canada has had a more moderate response, with legislative directives that encourage judges to use incarceration as a last resort. This book will explore the implications of our shifting response to crime, highlighting some alternatives that are in wide use but that receive less political and media attention. These examples will show that we should shift the debate away from considering policy as being either too "hard" or too "soft" on crime. This dichotomy distracts us from exploring effective and innovative responses to crime.

## Chapter 2

# Evaluating Criminal Justice System Responses

A society's response to crime reveals a great deal about its values. At one extreme, a totalitarian state responds to rule-breaking in an arbitrary way; the price of non-compliance is high, and the rules are often capricious, designed to control the population for political purposes. The state exerts control through fear. The criminal justice systems in most liberal democratic societies strive to balance the rights of victims and offenders, while drawing on a principled application of law and regulation. Citizens are aware of the rules and the consequences of breaking them.

Evaluating the goals of criminal justice, as well as how these goals may be best achieved, helps ensure that criminal justice policies adequately reflect our values and are implemented in a principled way. We should not be complacent about the criminal justice system's power to take away individual freedom.

This chapter examines the goals of the criminal justice system and considers how these goals both reflect and reinforce the values that underpin our particular social fabric in Canada. How do we justify inflicting punishment? How do we distribute punishment fairly? How do we know whether the justice system's response to crime is achieving the goals we want to achieve? This chapter evaluates the utilitarian goals of our justice system, including deterrence, rehabilitation, and incapacitation. It also considers the key debates over the principle of retribution.

## Goals

Public opinion polls have asked Canadians to identify the most important purpose of sentencing. The main goal—as ranked by the largest proportion of Canadians in several different surveys—is to require offenders to acknowledge and take responsibility for their crimes (Latimer and Desjardins 2007; Roberts, Crutcher, and Verbrugge 2007). The National Justice Survey asked Canadians to rate seven sentencing objectives. Accountability and reparation (making amends for a crime or paying compensation to a victim) were rated as "highly important" by more than 70 percent of respondents and rehabilitation by more than 60 percent (Latimer and Desjardins 2007). These findings suggest that Canadians want the justice system to juggle diverse goals.

These surveys ask questions about utilitarian goals. Utilitarianism requires that sanctions are imposed only if they result in positive outcomes, either for the individual or society. In this sense, utilitarian approaches are aimed at preventing future offences (Hudson 2003, 3). Utilitarian goals dominate the Canadian criminal justice responses to crime and are enshrined in the Principles of Sentencing included in the Criminal Code of Canada. Section 718 of the Criminal Code states that

> the fundamental purpose of sentencing is to contribute, along with crime prevention initiatives, to respect for the law and maintenance of a just, peaceful and safe society by imposing just sanctions that have one or more of the following objectives:
>
> 1. to denounce unlawful conduct;
> 2. to deter the offender and other persons from committing offences;
> 3. to separate offenders from society, where necessary;
> 4. to assist in rehabilitating offenders;
> 5. to promote reparations for harm done to victims or to the community; and
> 6. to promote a sense of responsibility in offenders, and acknowledgment of the harm done to victims and to the community.

These principles emerged from a large set of consultations and research in the late 1980s and early 1990s, and represented an effort to bring the purposes of sentencing in line with Canadian values. They also aimed to provide a balance of different objectives rather than prioritizing a single particular goal.[1]

The responses to crime are supported by different principles. For example, an emphasis on deterrence tends to underlie policies aimed at imposing harsher prison sentences; by contrast, an emphasis on reparation leads to responses more in line with restorative justice. Deterrence and rehabilitation, discussed below, attract widespread public and academic attention and are often used as measures of our system's success.

## Deterrence

The principle of deterrence is based on the assumption that we can discourage people from offending by imposing penalties or other negative consequences. Researchers who study the effects of deterrence distinguish between the certainty of punishment and the severity of punishment (von Hirsch et al. 1999). The certainty of punishment refers to the likelihood of being caught, found guilty, and punished. For example, many people would be less likely to park illegally if they were certain that they would be ticketed. Some criminal justice policies—such as increasing the number of police officers—might successfully influence the certainty of punishment. Other criminal justice polices aim to increase the severity of punishment. Policies to increase jail terms for specific crimes are one example of an effort to increase the severity of punishment. Many government policies assume that deterrence is effective and that increasing certainty or severity of punishment will reduce the crime rate.

Certainly, deterrence has some value and affects many of our day-to-day choices. Social norms may deter us from indulging in certain types of deviant or abnormal behaviour. Various regulations and bylaws also affect our choices. For example, many of us will drive around the block to find parking rather than risk a ticket. It may also be reasonable to think that the existence of the criminal justice system does have a generally deterring effect, and that without any system of penalty, we could expect to see more people choosing to commit certain types of crime. At the same time, however, there is reason to believe that deterrence is less effective than we might think.

Research suggests that the certainty of punishment has a more deterring effect than the severity of punishment (Gendreau et al. 1999; Smith, Goggin, and Gendreau 2002; von Hirsch et al. 1999). Indeed, most research produced in the last decade undermines the theory that more severe punishments result in more effective deterrence. One prominent Canadian criminologist, Anthony Doob, has concluded that we should accept the hypothesis that sentence severity has no effect on deterrence (Doob and Webster 2003). A survey of criminal justice experts in the US suggested a similar conclusion (Doob and Webster 2003). Even the widely read conservative criminologist James Q. Wilson has conceded that the US may have been overusing prisons as a means of deterring crime (Wilson 1995, cited in Doob and Webster 2003, 154). Given the body of research on this matter over the past three decades, it seems clear that policies that increase the severity of punishment are expensive—due to the high costs of imprisonment—and have little effect.

Deterrence theory is also based on several false assumptions. First is the belief that most crime is premeditated. A choice to park illegally is probably a fairly well-calculated decision. But many crimes happen quite spontaneously or in specific circumstances. As one criminologist has stated, people who commit crimes do not "rationally calculate with the same evaluative standards that legislators have, and partly because they live in a world already more foreboding than any prison, one which continually threatens street-imposed death penalties" (Skolnick 1995, 11). Second, deterrence can be effective only if potential criminals are up to date on the laws and sentencing practices. In an essay Anthony Doob discusses the decision of a Canadian court to increase the sentence of two women convicted of being drug mules. The court argued that it needed to "send a strong message" that such behaviours will not be tolerated. In his essay, Doob considers the extent to which potential drug mules might have paid attention to this case (Cayley 1998, 91). Elsewhere he notes that "in arguing that a three-year sentence will deter more people than a two-year sentence, one is suggesting that a measurable number of people would commit the offence with a reasonable expectation of serving a two-year sentence who would not do so if they thought that they would serve a three-year sentence" (Doob and Webster 2003, 190).

Implementing policies based on deterrence theory also comes up against a practical consideration. In order for deterrence to work, we must set sentences according to the most effective deterrents. We could probably never identify with any certainty exactly what punishments will effectively deter most potential offenders (Hudson 2003, 21). We could also never know if the same punishment will work in a similar way for all potential offenders.

We should consider a more principled argument about whether it is just to base our system of punishment on a principle of deterrence. General deterrence—the use of harsh punishment to deter future offenders—is particularly problematic. David Cayley notes that the moral objection to deterrence is that the person being punished is being treated as a means rather than an end (Cayley 1998, 90). Cayley adds that emphasizing deterrence is "even more unjust when we consider that members of marginalized groups are disproportionately involved with the criminal justice system. . . . These problems are associated with the way in which deterrence is a future-oriented response. Is it right, in other words, to inflict punishment based on something that might happen?" (Hudson 2003, 24).

Arguments for deterrence are often coupled with arguments for incapacitation. The Principles of Sentencing refer to incapacitation as "separating offenders from society." Confining offenders to custody will prevent them from offending with the most certainty. It may be a necessary response to some of the worst offenders and most serious offences (Hudson 2003, 32). In theory, then, incapacitation would work if we could identify and target the most high-risk repeat offenders (von Hirsch et al. 1999, 9). In reality, it has been difficult to make accurate predictions. Without knowing which offenders need to be taken out of society, incapacitation becomes a rather blunt instrument that results in over-incarceration of low-risk offenders. (Chapter 3 considers this issue in more detail.)

### Rehabilitation

Efforts to rehabilitate offenders are based on the assumption that the factors causing crime can be changed and that proper treatment will reduce offending and reoffending (Bonta et al. 2003; Hudson 2003). Rehabilitation is forward-looking, emphasizing the offender rather than the offence.

Past efforts at rehabilitation have met with limited success. During the early to mid-twentieth century, policies in Canada (and even more so in the US) focused on rehabilitation. In some American states, judges gave indeterminate sentences that would end only once the offender had been "cured." Such sentences were widely viewed as giving the state too much power over individuals; research also suggested that the treatment programs were inherently flawed and did not work (Martinson 1974). In a review of the literature produced during the mid-twentieth century, Martinson (1974) did not find evidence that rehabilitative programs used in prison reduced recidivism. He suggests that the programs were based on several false assumptions: that psychotherapy is effective, that educational and vocational programs are rehabilitative, and that the whole prison environment contributes to rehabilitation. The research on the failure of rehabilitation produced a backlash against utilitarian goals in the latter half of the century, particularly in the US (Alschuler 2003; Fish 2008). The American criminal justice system became retributive, an approach described in more detail in the next section of this chapter. Criminologists describe this time as the era when "nothing works."

In recent years, researchers with Correctional Service of Canada (CSC) have developed treatment models that appear to be quite effective. The models respond to offenders' risks, their individual needs, and their responsiveness to particular treatment (Bonta et al. 2003). The risk principle asserts that high-risk offenders should receive the most intensive treatment. Offenders' needs include psychological issues such as substance abuse or self-esteem. An offender's responsiveness relates to how open he or she may be to treatment or the potential success of specific approaches. Research suggests that treatment programs must target all three aspects of an offender: "An offender may be high risk and with clearly defined criminogenic needs, but treatment may have little impact if it is not delivered in a way that the offender can understand and that motivates him/her" (Bonta et al. 2003, 112). High-risk offenders benefit most from treatment, and it appears that community treatment programs may be more effective than those that are delivered in an institution (Andrews and Bonta 2006).

Effectiveness aside, rehabilitation models are not without their critics and potential risks. In the past, a heavy reliance on rehabilitative principles of sentencing has led to policies forcing offenders to demonstrate that they have been "cured" before they can be released (Hudson 2003, 29). At an extreme, this approach criminalizes the mentally ill, even for their involvement in minor offences, without providing them with the opportunity to seek appropriate treatment for their illness. We could also anticipate that offenders in custody could easily be coerced to participate in treatment programs (Law Commission of Canada 2003). We would then see very different sentences given out for similar crimes based only on the mental state of the offender rather than a principled stance about the seriousness of a particular crime. People with the most serious mental illnesses would therefore be punished the most severely. At a basic level, some critics also wonder whether it is right to frame offending as a "disease" that can be treated (Hudson 2003, 28). Some criminologists have further criticized Correctional Service of Canada's treatment model by arguing that it ignores gender differences and prioritizes victims' rights over offenders (Hannah-Moffat 2005; Marutto and Hannah-Moffat 2006; Ward, Melser, and Yates 2007).

## Distributing Punishment

Retribution is a principle that helps determine whether the severity of a punishment is proportionate to the seriousness of crime. Retribution is often associated with calls for punishment and revenge. This interpretation draws on the biblical tenet "an eye for an eye." Originally appearing in the sixteenth-century Code of Hammurabi, the idea of delivering punishment that is equivalent to the offence also appears in the Old Testament.

Retribution tends to drive calls for harsh punishment, including the death penalty, with no accounting for the offender's responsibility or criminal culpability (Alschuler 2003). In other words, the severity of punishment depends only on the seriousness of the crime, with no consideration of the circumstances. The punishment for theft would be the same regardless of the motivation. In this light, retribution fails to provide any rationale for punishment beyond the moral imperative to punish: "A retributivist believes that the imposition of deserved punishment is an intrinsic good" (Alschuler 2003).

Legal and religious scholars have debated the interpretation of the biblical tenet and have also questioned whether modern forms of retribution must inevitably lead to excessive punishment (Fish 2008, 69). In the Canadian Principles of Sentencing, retribution is presented as a means of restraining punishment to ensure that it is proportionate, but not necessarily equivalent, to the offence. It is not a goal in and of itself, but rather a principle to guide decisions about the severity of a punishment. According to Section 718.1 of the Principles of Sentencing in the Criminal Code, "A sentence must be proportionate to the gravity of the offence and the degree of responsibility of the offender." In other words, the punishment must fit the offence and the offender. It limits the extent to which a sentence may be used "to send a message" or as a means of ensuring that an offender is "cured." In this sense, then, it restrains judges from using excessive punishment as a means to achieve another end (such as deterrence).

## Social Values Reflected in Our Justice System

Retributive approaches, however, do overcome some of the problems associated with issuing punishment as a deterrent. Judges working in a retributive system where punishment is proportional will typically rely on sentencing guidelines that provide standard sentences for particular offences. Such guidelines prevent the application of a harsh sentence as a means of deterring some as-yet-unknown offence. The potential for future offending has no bearing on a sentence in a purely retributive system (Hudson 2003, 43). Retributive guidelines also prevent sentencing based on an offender's characteristics, such as race. In theory, then, a retributive system avoids race- or class-driven punishment (Hudson 2003, 46).

But retribution does not answer this question: How much punishment is enough? As with deterrence, it would be very difficult for us as a society to agree on how much punishment is proportionate to a given crime. How do we determine a properly proportionate sentence? We might easily agree on the most serious and least serious crimes— but probably not on the many others in between (Hudson 2003, 43). Even if we could come to some general agreement, restrictive sentencing guidelines can result in sentences that are unjust, because they remove a judge's discretion to consider the specific context of a given crime. On the one hand, this can result in harsh sentences for crimes that may appear on the surface to be quite similar but that are, on closer examination, quite different. On the other hand, a system based solely on proportionate retribution can eliminate judicial biases, such as race or class prejudice. In contrast to rehabilitation, retribution focuses only on the offence, punishing the same offence in the same way regardless of variations in the context or among the offenders. This is both its strength and its weakness.

## Values in Our Justice System

Retribution could be viewed as a value—we might believe that it is morally right to punish someone who has harmed someone else. A 2003 report by the Law Commission of Canada reveals other social values that come into play when we use the criminal justice system to respond to wrongdoing. The report's authors argue that we should assess our response to crime against concepts that are central to liberal democracies. These include justice, equality, accountability, and efficiency. Evaluating these concepts in relation to crime-control policies allows us to evaluate the underlying goals of criminal justice and, for that matter, why we should have such a system in the first place. Doing so can also shift our attention away from discussions of whether particular responses are "hard" or "soft" on crime and toward a discussion of what is really at stake: the rights and freedoms inherent in a liberal democratic society.

The concept of justice is tackled from different angles by philosophers, theologians, and legal scholars. For those interested in how we respond to crime, justice is sometimes equated with fairness and respect for rights. In other words, our criminal justice system should be fair and respectful. Although it may be difficult to achieve consensus on a particular criminal justice outcome, the system may still be seen as "just" if it does not abuse power or unduly remove freedoms that are intrinsic to our democratic principles. As the Law Commission states, "The authority to detain and punish is . . . an immense power within a liberal democratic society." We should also keep an eye on how our justice system deals with the social inequities that lead some people to commit crime and how well it works to counter, rather than reinforce, those inequities (Law Commission of Canada 2003, 37). The Law Commission's argument here is that we should strive to develop criminal justice policies that promote social as well as individual justice. Our social institutions must not replicate—and should work to obliterate—the social inequities that often arise between different groups. In the Law Commission's words, "Equality is at the core of our democratic society" (Law Commission of Canada 2003, 38).

In a society such as ours, citizens should be treated equally by the criminal justice system. No one group should be given preferential treatment or access to the resources required to defend themselves. Ideally, the justice system would be blind to race, class, gender, and other characteristics that distinguish social groups. In reality, the inequalities that permeate Canadian society are often carried into the justice system at all levels, including police, courts, and corrections. Given that two-thirds of those polled agreed—and almost half "strongly agreed"—that the justice system works best for those with money (Roberts 2004a), it seems that equality remains elusive.

Efficiency and accountability are also cornerstones of institutions in liberal democratic societies. Again, it is worth referring to the Law Commission: "accountability means that people exercising authority must account for the way in which they use their power within the public and private spheres. It also means that citizens should take responsibility for their conduct and the consequences of their actions" (Law Commission of Canada 2003, 40). In other words, the criminal justice system must hold offenders responsible for their actions, but should itself be answerable to the public at large for its operations. The system must also be efficient, not only in terms of cost (which is a key factor), but also in terms of priorities. For example, it costs a great deal of money to enforce the prohibition against possession of small amounts of marijuana. The relative harm of this crime may not warrant the cost of enforcing it. We noted above that increasing punishments is expensive and of limited efficacy. Policies that promote stiffer sentences may come at the expense of other social programs, such as health, education, and—ironically—crime prevention (Austin et al. 1999; Greenwood 1998). We should also avoid implementing policies that target social problems that the criminal justice system is poorly equipped to solve. Some crimes, such as drug abuse, may be better dealt with as health issues rather than criminal matters. "We deserve public policy that can achieve the results it promises," in the Law Commission's words (2003, 41).

## Evaluating Justice System Policies

The utilitarian goals discussed above are designed to produce results that can be measured. Reductions in crime rates, seriousness of crimes, and recidivism (or reoffending) are the most common measures of success. Deterrence, incapacitation, and rehabilitation should ideally produce those outcomes. Two key questions in evaluating the justice system are as follows: How much does incapacitation reduce the crime rate? And how much do rehabilitation programs reduce reoffending? (Later chapters explore these topics.)

To answer these questions we should start by looking at the statistics considered in Chapter 1 related to Canada's crime rate. Because it is largely derived from police statistics, the official crime rate is best seen as a measure of the volume of crimes reported to the police. We noted too in Chapter 1 that some crimes, such as sexual assault, are susceptible to under-reporting. And there are further complications. How much time should pass following the implementation of a given policy or program before a decrease in the crime rate might be expected? Could policies that target a particular crime actually increase its reporting to the police?

The limitations of research design are another barrier to a full understanding of effective policies. For example, research to assess whether an incapacitation policy decreases the crime rate is mired by many practical complications. Ideally, a policy would be implemented in one region and not another. Assuming the regions are similar in terms of crime, demographics, and other relevant characteristics, we would hope to see a change in crime rate in the area that applied the policy. Such an experimental design is routine in medical research but poses problems in social research. The first step would be to identify several communities that share similar characteristics such as crime rate, employment rate, demographics, and so on. But these variables cannot be easily controlled over the course of a study. For example, the communities may have similar rates of employment at the beginning of the study but a major change might take place—an employer might shut down over the course of the research, for example. Such a change could affect the crime rate independently of any program or policy.

While the process is not without its difficulties, it is still possible to design a study to test how a particular policy influences recidivism. Experimental treatment models can be tested on a random selection of offenders; these offenders can then be tracked for subsequent reoffending. Another group of offenders who do not receive the treatment can also be tracked by way of comparison. Retrospective research can also be conducted to look back at groups of offenders and their rates of recidivism with an eye to identifying the characteristics associated with lower levels of reoffending.

It is more difficult to design a study to test whether our efforts to deter, through a particular form of punishment, are effectively reducing rates of offending or reoffending. We could look at the pattern of punishments and assess whether harsh punishments affect the rate of offending. Again, this design is limited by how we determined which communities might be comparable, and how we avoid uncontrollable variables that can change the crime rate. In terms of reoffending, we might follow offenders post-release and ask them about their experiences of prison. Hypothetically, we could assess whether their experience of punishment is related to their subsequent patterns of reoffending. From the perspective of more general deterrence, researchers could explore the link between offenders' attitudes about punishment—whether they believed they would be caught and punished, whether they see the punishment for a particular crime to be harsh—and their offending patterns.

Another challenge associated with recidivism studies lies in measurement. While recidivism may be easy to define as "committing a crime following a previous conviction of a crime," it would be impossible to design research that can actually provide accurate statistics. We could rely on what are called self-report surveys that could ask convicted offenders to report on their subsequent activities. We might expect, however, that people with criminal records would be reluctant to report current offending, especially in a survey that might not be anonymous.

For this reason, measures of recidivism typically count only offences that come to the attention of the criminal justice system. Some studies look at contact with the police as recidivism. Others look only at an arrest or a conviction as an instance of reoffending. Reconviction is becoming the standard measure of recidivism (Farrington and Davies 2007). The problem with this approach is that very few crimes come to the attention of the criminal justice system. Fewer still result in a conviction. As a result, recidivism numbers will always underestimate how much crime is being committed by those who have already been convicted of an offence.

Once a clear definition has been established, we must then determine what researchers refer to as the "level of measurement." This involves the following question: Do we treat recidivism as a dichotomy (that someone either reoffended or they did not) or as a continuum (by looking at the number of re-offences)? We might also ask if crimes committed by a given individual are becoming less serious over time, indicating a diminution if not a complete cessation of offending. As a result of this dilemma, the success of a program aimed to reduce recidivism depends on how we define success: Is it a complete cessation of crime, or less offending and less serious offences? Over what period of time do we want to measure recidivism?

Clearly, the definitions and decisions about measurement will have a dramatic effect on the numbers produced. A study that defines recidivism narrowly as reconviction and follows offenders for a short period of time will find less recidivism than a study that defines recidivism more broadly and follows offenders for a longer period of time. Chapter 3 will describe some of these differences in more detail.

Questions about evaluating utilitarian goals revolve around measuring the effects of our efforts to deter, incapacitate, and rehabilitate. Subsequent chapters of this book will evaluate the various ways that we respond to crime by measuring whether they achieve utilitarian goals.

To explore retribution we need to look elsewhere. Crime rates and recidivism statistics will not tell us whether the harshness of a sentence is proportionate to the harm of the crime. Some American states have developed sentencing formulas: using a mathematical formula, judges determine the sentence based on the offender's characteristics and the nature of the offence. While judges have some discretion in how they weigh aspects of an individual case, this system is highly retributive, insofar as sentences are prescribed by very tight guidelines. With no such system in place in Canada, we might look at actual sentencing patterns to determine if sentences are harsher for crimes that we consider more serious. We might ask offenders about how difficult it was to complete a particular sentence. Or we might rely on public opinion to determine punishments that fit different crimes. Either way, we would expect not to agree on the relative seriousness of various punishments, or the reactions to particular crimes or specific offenders. Subsequent chapters of this book will look at each type of criminal justice response and assess the extent to which it is proportionate to the crimes.

## Chapter 3

# Imprisonment

The earliest prisons were places to confine criminals awaiting trial or corporal punishment. The use of prisons for rehabilitation or public protection is a relatively recent development, emerging from the penitentiaries and reformatories of the mid-nineteenth century. In the twenty-first century, prisons are now seen as institutions that can protect public safety.

Like many Western democracies, Canada's prison system has emerged out of this historical background. The mission statement of Correctional Service of Canada (CSC), the agency that runs federal prisons, reflects the multiple goals of a modern prison system:

> The Correctional Service of Canada, as part of the criminal justice system and respecting the rule of law, contributes to public safety by actively encouraging and assisting offenders to become law-abiding citizens, while exercising reasonable, safe, secure and humane control.

The public endorses this balance of rehabilitation and public safety. A 1997 poll found that 37 percent of Canadians saw public protection as the primary goal of prisons. A slightly smaller proportion, 34 percent, chose rehabilitation. These goals are very utilitarian, to recall the concept introduced in Chapter 2. Only 17 percent of Canadians chose punishment as the central purpose of prisons. In recent years, however, political and public debates have begun to focus on retributive punishment as a distinct goal that the prison system should aim to achieve.

Indeed, we may be witnessing a shift away from the traditional balance of rehabilitation and public safety toward an emphasis on prisons as punishment. The "transformative agenda," currently being implemented by CSC, illustrates this shift. The changes are being guided by an extensive report, *A Roadmap to Strengthening Public Safety*, produced by the CSC Review Panel in 2007. The independent panel, appointed by the Conservative government to review corrections in Canada, argued for a dramatic shift in the operation of prisons in Canada.[1] The report asserts that prisons should be used as punishment, and that prison sentences should involve a series of rewards for good behaviour and punishments for bad (Correctional Service of Canada Review Panel 2007). Conservative MPs applauded the report; former Justice Minister Vic Toews, for example, stated in a speech to the Canadian Professional Police Association: "I believe that it is time to get tough when it comes to incarcerating violent offenders, and I applaud the efforts that have been made to put an end to what has been referred to as 'Club Fed'" (Toews 2006).

The legislative changes outlined in Chapter 1 (such as the changes in rules around credit for time served awaiting sentence) also demonstrate that our reliance on prisons will be increasing. This chapter evaluates the use of prison against the utilitarian goals and retributive principles outlined in the previous chapter. The current chapter begins with an overview of the Canadian prison system, considering both the federal and provincial systems and exploring the successes and failures of the system in terms of programming, living conditions, and recidivism. An evaluation of the Correctional Services Canada's "transformative agenda" considers the shift toward offender accountability, through rewards and punishments. Is this approach supported by research? What kinds of social values are reflected in this move?

## Canada's Prison System

The Canadian prison system is administered by two levels of government. Across Canada, provincial and territorial governments run just over one hundred custodial facilities. The federal government, through CSC, oversees upwards of 57 institutions, including five Aboriginal healing lodges and five institutions that house only women. Offenders convicted of summary offences—which are among the least serious crimes and have maximum prison sentences of six months or less—serve time in a provincial or territorial jail. Those convicted of an indictable offence may be sent either to a federal or a provincial institution. If a sentence is less than two years, the offender serves time in a provincial or territorial jail. Offenders sentenced to two years or more go to a federal prison.

Federal penitentiaries have the most intensive programs and the highest levels of security. CSC supervises fewer offenders, serving longer sentences, than the provinces and territories (Calverley 2010). In 2008–9,

## Profile of Federal Inmates

Age: The average age for people admitted to federal jurisdiction was thirty-three in 2005–2006. This has since increased slightly. Aboriginal offenders tend to be younger than non-Aboriginal offenders.

Gender: Of those admitted to federal custody, 6 percent are women.

Ethnicity: 17 percent of inmates admitted are Aboriginal (compared with 4 percent of the Canadian population who identify themselves as Aboriginal).

Marital Status: 60 percent of inmates are single or never married.

Education: About half of inmates have some secondary education; one-third have completed secondary; few have any post-secondary education.

Addictions: 80 percent of people enter a federal penitentiary with a substance abuse problem.

Offences: One-quarter of offenders are serving time in a federal penitentiary for homicide; one-third for robbery; one sixth for sexual offences; one-quarter for drugs.

Source: Landry and Sinha 2008

for example, only 2 percent of offenders admitted to custody in Canada were sent to a federal prison, while 63 percent were sent to a provincial/territorial institution, either to serve their sentence or to be held on remand while awaiting trial or sentence hearing. The rest were supervised in the community. Overall, provincial sentences are typically just over one month, with a high of 62 days in Newfoundland and Labrador to a low of 17 days in Ontario (Calverley 2010).[2] Excluding those serving life sentences, offenders in federal custody typically spend a year and a half in prison. Almost one-quarter of the federal prison population is serving a life or indeterminate sentence.[3] Most are incarcerated, but about one-third are under community supervision.

Federal and provincial/territorial institutions serve different inmate populations. All inmates in federal custody have been convicted of a crime and sentenced to a period of incarceration. In provincial institutions just under half are serving a custodial sentence ordered by a judge. The rest are on remand, awaiting court hearings such as trials.[4] On any given day just over thirteen thousand inmates are serving a sentence in a federal prison. Another seven thousand offenders are being supervised by CSC in the community. Inmates being held in provincial custody have been convicted of less serious crimes than those held in federal prisons. The majority, 69 percent, of federal offenders are serving time for a violent crime. Of those, just under one-third have been convicted of murder. In provincial institutions fewer than one-quarter of inmates have been convicted of a violent crime (Babooram 2008). A larger proportion of federal offenders are serving time for drug-related offences compared to provincial offenders.

Reconviction rates for inmates released from both federal and provincial institutions are fairly high. CSC followed all federal offenders released for one year in the mid-1990s, and found that almost half were reconvicted of a crime within two years following their release. Women were less likely to be reconvicted than men. Those who had been jailed for a violent offence were less likely to be reconvicted than those who had been previously convicted of a property offence. Aboriginal offenders had a higher rate of reconviction than non-Aboriginal offenders (Bonta, Dauvergne, and Rugge 2003). We have good data from Ontario showing that in 2004–5, 40 percent of offenders released from provincial prisons returned within six months, convicted of a new offence. Unfortunately, the data do not reveal if these convictions were for new offences, committed after the offenders were released from jail, or for offenses committed prior to the first jail sentence (Ministry of Community Safety and Correctional Services 2008). We also cannot tell whether provincial or federal inmates are more likely to reoffend because the time frames used for each group differed.

The profile of those serving time in federal penitentiaries has changed in the past decade (Babooram 2008). The proportion of federal inmates serving time for violent crimes has decreased from 58 percent in 1997–98 to 49 percent in 2006–7. The proportion of inmates convicted of drug offences has decreased slightly, from 14 percent in 1997–98 to 11 percent in 2006–7. Federal prisons now include more people serving time for property offences and other offences that include probation breaches. These shifts indicate a less high-risk or dangerous inmate population. However, these changes may be offset by other equally significant changes to the inmate population. Federal prisons now admit more inmates who are affiliated with gangs, and an increasing number of inmates suffer from mental health and addiction problems (Correctional Service of Canada Review Panel 2007). The rate of incarceration of Aboriginal offenders is a cause for concern. Not only has the incarceration rate for Aboriginal peoples increased in recent years (from 815 per 100,000 in 2001 to 983 per 100,000 in 2006), it is nine times higher than the overall incarceration rate (Landry and Sinha 2008).

# Aboriginal Inmates

People who identify themselves as Aboriginal are disproportionately represented in Canada's prisons. Seventeen percent of inmates in Canada are Aboriginal whereas only 4 percent of the adult population identify as such. The proportion of Aboriginal inmates varies across the provinces, and the problem of over-representation is exacerbated in provinces with larger Aboriginal populations. In Manitoba, for example, 16 percent of the population identify as Aboriginal compared to 71 percent of people admitted to prison.

In 2006, Howard Sapers, Canada's Correctional Investigator, released a report that highlighted how Canadian Aboriginal people suffer discrimination in Canada's correctional system (Correctional Investigator 2006). He pointed out that they are disproportionately classified as high risk. As a result, more Aboriginal inmates are sent to higher security prisons that have fewer rehabilitative programs and are more centrally located, making them further away from inmates' communities and local support networks. This problem is exacerbated for female Aboriginal inmates. The Correctional Investigator also found that Aboriginal inmates are placed in segregation more often than non-Aboriginals and that their parole applications are less likely to succeed.

A closer look at the Aboriginal inmate population reveals some key differences from the rest of the prison population. In provincial institutions the reasons for incarceration are similar to those of non-Aboriginal offenders. In federal custody, however, Aboriginal inmates are disproportionately serving time for a violent offence. CSC assessments suggest that Aboriginals enter custody with more problems relating to family, employment, and addictions than non-Aboriginal offenders. For example, according to these assessments, 93 percent of Aboriginal inmates have a substance abuse problem, compared to 78 percent of the rest of the inmate population. These characteristics do not even begin to reflect the wider social context that finds disproportionate amounts of poverty and social problems among Aboriginal people.

The gaps between Aboriginal and non-Aboriginal inmates persist despite years of efforts to address this issue. Since the mid-1990s, CSC has worked with Aboriginal communities to develop policies and to implement culturally specific programs, such as healing lodges (Correctional Service of Canada 2009b). Despite these efforts, many commentators—including those who are generally supportive of the work done by correctional institutions—are critical of the lack of change. For example, the Correctional Service Review Panel reports that there has been little action, despite years of analysis (Correctional Service of Canada Review

## The View from the Court

In 1996, an amendment to the Criminal Code instructed judges to consider all alternatives to prison when imposing a sentence, particularly in cases involving Aboriginal offenders. In a landmark case in 1999, the Supreme Court of Canada directed judges to consider:

> (a) the unique systemic or background factors which may have played a part in bringing the particular aboriginal offender before the courts; and (b) the types of sentencing procedures and sanctions which may be appropriate in the circumstances for the offender because of his or her particular aboriginal heritage or connection. In order to undertake these considerations the sentencing judge will require information pertaining to the accused. Judges may take judicial notice of the broad systemic and background factors affecting aboriginal people, and of the priority given in aboriginal cultures to a restorative approach to sentencing. In the usual course of events, additional case-specific information will come from counsel and from a pre-sentence report which takes into account the systemic or background factors and the appropriate sentencing procedures and sanctions, which in turn may come from representations of the relevant aboriginal community.

Source: R. v. Gladue [1999] 1 S.C.R. 688[5]

Panel 2007). The Correctional Investigator of Canada, Howard Sapers, has also expressed impatience at the lack of progress (Correctional Investigator 2009).

This lack of progress continues despite a major legislative change in 1996 with the introduction of Section 718.2(e) to the Criminal Code. This section directs judges to consider alternatives to imprisonment, particularly for Aboriginal offenders. It allows judges to apply sanctions that more closely match traditional values and to consider the history of colonialism and marginalization that has produced the context for much of Aboriginal offending. Ultimately, this amendment aims to reduce the over-incarceration of Aboriginal offenders. That the trend is ongoing suggests that we have not yet found the right balance of punishment and justice for the Aboriginal population. The data suggest that we need a wholesale review of how the criminal justice system treats Aboriginals.

## Mental Illness

Mental health issues are among the biggest challenges faced by correctional institutions in Canada today (Correctional Investigator 2009). The percentage of offenders who are admitted to federal custody with a mental illness has doubled in the past five years; the proportion of inmates with prescriptions for mental health–related medication has doubled in the past decade. One study of a sample of offenders in an Edmonton jail found that the inmates were more than twice as likely as members of the general population to have had a recent psychiatric illness. The inmates were also seven times more likely to have attempted suicide (Bland et al. 1990). These numbers suggest that mental health services should be a central part of correctional programs.

Mental illnesses create difficulties for incarcerated individuals and pose considerable institutional challenges as well. As Olley suggests, inmates with mental illnesses "can present a risk of harm to themselves or others," and they create "management challenges for staff and a liability concern for decision-makers" (Olley, Nicholls, and Brink 2009). They also commit rule violations that lead to segregation or other forms of protective custody that serve to exacerbate the mental illness (Correctional Investigator 2009). Nor is the prison environment conducive to their recovery:

> It is hard to conceive of a less helpful environment for a person facing serious mental illness than a federal prison. At its best, it is a place that engenders fear, defensiveness, denial, stigmatization and isolation. At its worst it becomes a segregation cell that can put relatively healthy people into psychotic states. Compounding the problems are the additional factors that many seriously mentally ill are without family support while in prison and outside community resources are often not available. (Jackson and Stewart 2009, 11)

The situation is a worst-case scenario for both inmate recovery and the safety and security of everyone living or working in the institution. Craig Jones, director of the John Howard Society, writes:

> [when] we are talking about federally incarcerated prisoners, we are talking about multi-stigmatized persons, the large percentage of whom come to the prison system with untreated trauma, mental illness of some kind, very often a developmental disability, and criminality. We layer on to these people various forms of stigmatization, and then when we release them into the community, which is another issue altogether, we wonder why they fail. We restigmatize them and restigmatize them and restigmatize them. (Jones 2009)

In an effort to deal with mental illness in Canadian prisons, and in response to the CSC Review Panel, CSC hired new staff with expertise in mental illnesses. They have also trained existing staff and developed partnerships in the community and improved mental health screening of inmates. Despite these efforts, however, problems remain. The Correctional Investigator (2009, 7) argues that mental health services are inadequate and this results in prisons essentially "warehousing" people with mental illness while not having any effect on public safety. The ongoing failure of CSC to meet the needs of inmates suffering from mental illnesses is particularly troubling in light of the fact that the problem was highlighted in 2007 by the CSC Review Panel.

The failures are tragically illustrated in the case of Ashley Smith. Smith spent three years in provincial custody; her sentence was continually increased due to offences she committed while in custody. These offences, according to the Correctional Investigator, were a result of altercations between Smith and correctional staff who were responding to her self-harming behaviours. Much of her time in custody was spent in segregation. In 2006, Smith was transferred to a federal prison to serve an adult sentence for another incident involving an altercation between her and correctional staff, who were ill-prepared to deal with mental illness. Over the next year, Ashley Smith was often held in segregation,

## The View from Ashley Smith

This poem was written in the New Brunswick Youth Centre when Ashley Smith was 16 or 17 years old. She was detained there for 36 months, 27 of which she spent in a form of segregation known as "temporary quiet."

### My Life

**By Ashley Smith**

My life I no longer love
I'd rather be set free above
Get it over with while the time is right
Late some rainy night
Turn black as the sky and as cold as the sea
Say goodbye to Ashley
Miss me but don't be sad
I'm not sad I'm happy and glad
I'm free, where I want to be
No more caged up Ashley
Wishing I were free
Free like a bird.

Source: New Brunswick Ombudsman and Child and Youth Advocate 2008

in a room alone, with no clothing other than a smock, no mattress and no blanket. She often slept on the floor. In October 2007, Smith killed herself in her prison cell while being watched by correctional staff who had been ordered not to intervene unless she stopped breathing. The Correctional Investigator has pointed to the many failures of the system that led to Ashley Smith's death (Correctional Investigator 2008b). Many of the failures were associated with the inability of correctional staff to address the needs of mentally ill offenders.[6]

The case of Ashley Smith had an extreme outcome, but the lack of care that led to her death is systemic and pervasive (Correctional Investigator 2008a; Correctional Investigator 2008b; Correctional Investigator 2009). Just before her death, she spoke of her desire to commit suicide; however, she did not receive adequate or immediate medical care when she wrapped a ligature around her neck. This case raises particular concerns about the use of segregation to manage offenders who are suffering from mental illnesses. According to the Correctional Investigator of Canada, the incidents preceding Smith's death were not isolated events. Her case illustrates that without the appropriate treatment for their mental health problems, inmates are a high risk to both themselves and to others.

## Drugs

First-person accounts from inmates suggest that drugs are widely available in Canadian correctional institutions (Small et al. 2005). CSC reports that 8 percent of inmates tested positive for drug use during random drug tests in 2008–9, the same rate as in the previous year (Correctional Service of Canada 2009a). CSC also reports that 40 percent of inmates surveyed reported having used illegal drugs while incarcerated, 11 percent of them with needles (Robinson and Mirabelli 1995). Substance abuse in prison is a clear cause for concern.

Drugs in prison lead to transmission of disease, through shared needles, and injuries to inmates. One study of inmates in seven provincial prisons in Canada found that just over 2 percent of male and almost 9 percent of female inmates were HIV positive. Almost all of those who were HIV positive were injection drug users. Similarly, Hepatitis C virus infections were associated with intravenous drug use: half of male and more than half of the female injection drug users were infected (Poulin et al. 2008). The rate of HIV and Hepatitis C infections in jails is about 20 percent higher among the inmate population than in the general population. Almost one-quarter of the 152 serious injuries in prisons for 2009–10 were caused by overdoses (Correctional Service of Canada

# The View from Inside

Will Small is a Canadian researcher who has documented stories from people living in Canadian prisons. One inmate reports on the dangers of drug use:

> It's a nightmare. Equipment like syringes are in very, very short supply. You see syringes that have literally been around for months and months, if not years . . . patched and repaired, used over and over and over and over again. I am sure that many, many cases of HIV were transmitted because of those practices . . . sharing. Everybody shares.

Another participant in Small's research states that:

> Drug addicts in jail are incredibly inventive. I have seen people actually, literally manufacture syringes out of pens. You know, pen bodies for the barrel, and maybe they've got a very old syringe that they've cut off right down, very close to the point and somehow glued on, or attached for the point.

Source: Small et al. 2005, 836

2010b). These statistics reveal the serious consequences of failing to address the problem of drug use in prisons.

Harm reduction, discussed in Chapter 6, is widely accepted to be the best way to reduce the spread of illnesses related to drug use. Methadone programs, needle exchange programs, and the provision of bleach kits to sterilize needles are the most common approaches. According to research cited by CSC, harm reduction lessens the problems associated with drug use; moreover, it has not been found to lead to an increase in drug use. CSC research also reveals that methadone maintenance programs have reduced recidivism rates (Griffiths, Dandurand, and Murdoch 2007). Canadian prisons have bleach kits and some offer methadone programs. None have implemented a needle exchange program; research also suggests that inmates have found it difficult to access and use bleach kits (Chu and Peddle 2010). Even so, CSC does have an explicit commitment to harm reduction in Canadian prisons, and a recent directive from the Commissioner has reiterated that harm-reduction items should be readily available (Commissioner of the Correctional Service of Canada 2009).

Despite the promise of harm-reduction programs, the CSC Review Panel focused on controlling drugs with security and surveillance. Their report makes no mention of harm reduction. How these recommendations will affect CSC policy is not clear, but moving toward a

# The View of a Correctional Officer

Jeff Doucette was a correctional officer and head of the Emergency Response Team at Millhaven Prison. He has witnessed many suicides and murders, and the stress eventually led him to quit:

You try and put [these things] away, you try and keep distracted, you try and keep busy, you try and do a lot of things. But of myself, the best I can describe it is that, at its worst, you're waking up with nightmares. I used to have this film that played. It was like I was watching a screen in front of me, and I'd be talking to you, and it would be through all these bodies and blood and situations. And these played, non-stop, fifteen years of them. And you can't function all that long. You sleep two hours a night, because the nightmares are bad, and when you wake up you just sit and smoke cigarettes or something, because you're not going back to sleep. That's just not an option at the time, right? It's easier to be awake, I guess. And it doesn't take too long before you're exhausted. ...

And the worst problem is that, when you've worked there ten, fifteen, twenty years, whatever, you take that as normal. That's your normal daily fare. I've had a chance to sit back and look at it and it's not normal. . . . I was pumping adrenalin twenty-four hours a day, severely depressed, just nonfunctional.

Source: Cayley 1998, 115

security-oriented approach is failing to take research into account and potentially undermines the progress that CSC has made in terms of harm reduction. Certainly CSC's own performance report notes no decrease in the number of positive tests in 2008–9, after the implementation of the security-type measures recommended by the panel.

## Conditions in Canadian Prisons

Drug use and mental illness contribute to the negative environment faced by both inmates and staff in Canadian correctional institutions. The Correctional Investigator has complained about the living conditions in Canadian prisons. In one visit to a maximum security institution, an investigator noted several troubling conditions and situations, including:

- Cell lock-up of inmates not attending programs or work;
- Meals confined to cells;
- Lengthy lock-downs of entire ranges to facilitate population movement through the institution;

## The Case against Segregation

Based on his work in Canadian prisons, the Correctional Investigator has argued that segregation is both counterproductive, in terms of changing inmate behaviour, and inhumane. In his 2008–9 report he argues that depriving inmates of human contact can only exacerbate mental illness and run counter to achieving rehabilitation. He also suggests that his investigations show that inmates with mental health problems are being put into segregation for behaviors associated with their illnesses. He states that: "[t]he practice of confining offenders with mental disorder to prolonged periods of isolation and deprivation must end. It is not safe, nor is it humane" (Correctional Investigator 2009, 16).

- A high number of "exceptional" searches;
- No association between inmates from different living ranges;
- Restricted access to the recreation yard, the gym, and daily fresh-air exercise;
- Excessive restrictions on visits;
- Unclean and noisy common areas, including the gym, showers, and yard;
- A high number of overdue complaints and grievances.

The 2008–9 Annual Report of the Correctional Investigator reported "serious concerns about the overall mood, health, and culture of the institutions, deeming the environments stressful, restless, tense, and unsafe for both inmates and staff." The investigator also complained about the over-use of segregation (Correctional Investigator 2009, 34). These descriptions defy the characterization of Canadian prisons as "Club Fed."

Not only can conditions be poor, but inmates experience a high level of victimization. Officially, CSC reported 560 assaults committed by inmates on other inmates in 2008–9 (Correctional Service of Canada 2009a), a victimization rate of just under 3 percent. A victimization survey of inmates from 1993 found a much higher rate of violence and victimization. The study found that almost half of the prisoners interviewed had been victimized in some way in the 12 months prior to the interview. Many reported more than one occasion of victimization. Theft accounted for 20 percent and assault for 28 percent of the incidents. Weapons were present in one-third of victimizations. The victimization rate for men in prison was more than twice the rate for men of comparable ages in the general population (Cooley 1993; Correctional Investigator 2006).

## The View of a Correctional Officer

Jeff Doucette was a correctional officer and head of the Emergency Response Team at Millhaven Prison. He has witnessed many suicides and murders, and the stress eventually led him to quit:

> You try and put [these things] away, you try and keep distracted, you try and keep busy, you try and do a lot of things. But of myself, the best I can describe it is that, at its worst, you're waking up with nightmares. I used to have this film that played. It was like I was watching a screen in front of me, and I'd be talking to you, and it would be through all these bodies and blood and situations. And these played, non-stop, fifteen years of them. And you can't function all that long. You sleep two hours a night, because the nightmares are bad, and when you wake up you just sit and smoke cigarettes or something, because you're not going back to sleep. That's just not an option at the time, right? It's easier to be awake, I guess. And it doesn't take too long before you're exhausted. ...
>
> And the worst problem is that, when you've worked there ten, fifteen, twenty years, whatever, you take that as normal. That's your normal daily fare. I've had a chance to sit back and look at it and it's not normal. . . . I was pumping adrenalin twenty-four hours a day, severely depressed, just nonfunctional.

Source: Cayley 1998, 115

Correctional officers have also been implicated in acts of prison violence, although little information is publicly available on the use of force by correctional officials against inmates (Correctional Investigator 2006). In 2004, CSC reported that guards used force about one thousand times (Correctional Investigator 2006). In 2009–10 that number increased to 1,372 (Correctional Service of Canada 2010d). A higher proportion of inmates suffered injuries from these incidents (Correctional Service of Canada 2010d).[7]

The number of injuries of both guards and inmates has been going down, but the numbers are still alarming. In 2009–10, 2,258 injuries were reported, involving 1,656 different inmates or 8 percent of the prison population. About half the injuries were sustained in fights between inmates or other assaults. Twenty percent of injuries were self-inflicted (Correctional Service of Canada 2010b). It should be noted that guards are also at risk: CSC reported 265 assaults on staff by inmates in 2008–9. Guards, like inmates, also suffer the stress of witnessing violence in prisons: "They bear the scars of imprisonment as surely as their prisoners" (Cayley 1998).

# Programs in Canadian Prisons

Some commentators have noted that prison does not offer an environ-ment that is conducive to self-improvement (Cayley 1998). Others have pointed out the irony of encouraging an inmate to change his or her life in the absence of freedom:

> We expect that when someone is released from prison he will have "learned his lesson." But how can an individual learn to act re-sponsibly in an environment which strips him of the freedom to make significant decisions about the course of his own life? (John Howard Society of Ontario, n.d.)

Presumably, however, the prison system aims to provide programs to counter the effects of imprisonment, as well as to facilitate an inmate's ability to address the issues that have led him or her to offend in the first place.

Correctional Service of Canada is required to provide programs to inmates that will address the causes of their offending and help pre-vent their reoffending later. Upon admission to prison, inmates are assessed and a correctional plan is developed. This plan outlines the programs and activities that CSC believes will contribute to rehabilita-tion. Successful completion of programs affects inmates' eligibility for parole. Program areas include:

- Living skills
- Violence prevention
- Substance abuse prevention
- Family violence prevention
- Sex offender treatment
- Employment readiness

Source: Public Safety Canada 2007

CORCAN, a rehabilitative program of CSC, is one of the largest pro-grams offered, providing training to help federal offenders gain skills that will enable their entry into the job market. Approximately four thousand inmates go through the program each year, learning basic skills, personal management, and teamwork. Inmates are trained and employed in five businesses (agribusiness, textiles, manufacturing, construction, and the service industry). Adult Basic Education is anoth-er critical component of prison programs, responding to the fact that 70 percent of inmates have not completed high school (Correctional

Service of Canada Review Panel 2007). Programs, sometimes delivered in collaboration with Aboriginal communities, have also been created to help Aboriginal inmates. With all of these programs, the goal is to protect society by helping inmates address some of the issues that may be related to their offending.

The rehabilitative and treatment programs from the CSC are among the best in the world. Their evidence-based programs are designed and modified based on research. Despite this reputation, both the Correctional Investigator of Canada and the Correctional Service of Canada Review Panel express concerns about programming. The panel complains specifically about low participation and completion rates (Correctional Service of Canada Review Panel 2007). Most programs have completion rates of between 60 and 75 percent: sex offender programs have the lowest rates, while life skills programs have the highest. In the past, programs for female offenders have had high completion rates, but these have dropped in recent years. Programs for Aboriginal inmates have among the lowest completion rates. The report does not offer an explanation for these numbers but the lack of inmate participation and completion detracts from their potential.

Two years following complaints by *A Roadmap to Strengthening Public Safety*, CSC reported a general increase in the number of offenders participating in and completing programs (Correctional Service of Canada 2009a). In 2009, however, the Correctional Investigator reported that only 2 percent of the more than two-billion-dollar budget allocated to CSC is spent on programs. He also reported that less than 25 percent of the prison population is participating in "core" correctional programs (Correctional Investigator 2010). Given the importance of programs, this appears to be a disproportionately small allocation of funds.

According to the Correctional Investigator, some offenders have no access to programs as they are not available in all institutions. In fact, the Correctional Investigator cites cases in which offenders are not eligible to apply for parole because of the lack of availability. Not only is this unfair to inmates, it also fails to ensure public safety: offenders have not been properly reintegrated into the community. More offenders are serving their full sentence inside of prisons—without proper programs—only to be released at the end of their sentence without any support or oversight from CSC. As the Correctional Investigator (2009) has suggested, offenders need programs in order to ensure that they will be able to live in a law-abiding way once they are released. Despite these criticisms, the Correctional Investigator of Canada is hopeful that a $48.8 million Strategic Review, currently underway, will allow for increased funds to be allocated to programs.

## The View from Inside

Writing in the *Journal of Prisoners on Prisons*, Dan Cahill describes how

few criminals are "hardened" when they enter the prison system, since the majority of prisoners start out as non-violent offenders. We become inured to the degradation and punishment handed down by the criminal justice system. It is the system itself which hardens a criminal in most cases. The hardened offender becomes increasingly indifferent to the suffering and loss inflicted upon the victim, which enable an offender to commit even more serious and harmful offences. It is important to understand this apathy because it is the shield criminals use to avoid facing the pain or loss inflicted on their victims . . . .The ability to ignore and be indifferent to the plight of the less fortunate is all too obvious in our society. It is the same shield we all use to avoid facing the pain and loss our actions (or inactions) inflict on others.

Source: Cahill 1998, 1

What is not clear is how the government will respond to the criticism about poor access to programming. The CSC Review Panel suggests that incentives should be put in place encouraging inmates to complete programs. In 2009, former Public Safety Minister Peter Van Loan stated that "the government wants to create an incentive system for prisoners to participate in rehabilitation programs" (Van Loan 2009a). He suggested that inmates should not be eligible for statutory release, which requires that offenders serve the last third of their sentence in the community if they have not completed rehabilitative programs. While this option may seem attractive, the reality is that most offenders will be released at some point, and those offenders who serve part of their sentence in the community, on probation or parole, have better outcomes. If the availability of statutory release is limited, then more offenders will be released at the end of the sentence, without the benefit of an easing back into community life. As stated on the Public Safety web page, "Almost all inmates will be released from custody eventually. The best way to protect society is through the safe, gradual, and structured return of offenders to the community" (Public Safety Canada 2009b).

## Evaluating Canada's Prison System

Clearly the one thing that imprisonment does accomplish is incapacitation; incarcerated offenders cannot commit crimes. One American pundit memorably pointed out that, "A thug in prison cannot shoot your sister" (Wattenberg 1993, 14). While this statement is undeniably true, it does not form the basis of sound policy for several reasons. The thug is unlikely to be imprisoned indefinitely. Also most offenders are young men, and imprisoning all men when they reach a given age is no solution: first, the new generation will be free to commit crimes; second, the previous generation, as it matures, will no longer pose the same threat to society as it did when its members were of a more high-risk age, and therefore will not require the same level of incapacitation.

The experience in the US is telling. Many American states adopted incapacitation polices—such as the notorious "three strikes" policy in California—in the late twentieth century. The policies resulted in prisons overcrowded with large numbers of people convicted of minor offences.[8] Furthermore, it is difficult to attribute the drop in some types of crime in the US to incapacitation, given that other Western countries, including Canada, have had similar drops without the same policies. Indeed, in Canada, we sentence fewer offenders to imprisonment. This suggests that incapacitation, in the form of lengthy jail terms, does not affect the crime rate. Given the American experience, it is not at all clear that large-scale incarceration of offenders for relatively minor crimes is either just or efficient.

Research also suggests that an increased use of imprisonment does not improve recidivism rates. Many studies over the years have looked into the relationship between types of criminal justice sanctions and recidivism or reoffending. In recent years, researchers have used this large body of literature to conduct studies that compare the results of various research projects and identify common findings. The results of this work suggest that prison does not reduce criminal behaviour and in some cases may increase it (Smith, Goggin, and Gendreau 2002). Other research has shown that increasing the security level of prisons can lead to higher rates of recidivism (Gaes and Camp 2009; Smith, Goggin, and Gendreau 2002). While prison may incapacitate in the short term, it may do more harm than good for a large number of offenders in the long term.

The American experience of mass incarceration and the research literature on recidivism provide us with strong evidence that incapacitation should be used, as the Canadian Principles of Sentencing suggest, only "where necessary"—that is, for the most persistent, most violent offenders. The question then is this: Which offenders should be incarcerated? Jim Cavanagh, who served time in Canadian prisons before becoming Director of the Kingston chapter of the Prison Fellowship Ministry, questioned how many inmates really do need to be behind bars to protect public safety (Cayley 1998).

in all prisons across Canada, there's only a handful in each prison that need to be detained behind the walls. The rest of them can be out in some sort of community-work program or some alternative thing. They don't need to be warehoused. But the thing is you're in a dilemma. You have a lot of people in society who are angry over a lot of issues, so when crime comes into the picture they're just saying, "lock 'em up and throw the key away"; and they don't realize that by using that stance and that attitude, they're compounding and escalating crime in Canada. They're making it worse. Instead of saying, "Hey, I'm the taxpayer. What is being done to change these individuals and make them responsible for their actions? And what's being done to help the victims monetarily, and also to restore a relationship between the victim and the offender to find out, hey, how did you do this to me?" (cited in Cayley 1998, 106)

Research shows that prison programs are needed to offset the negative effects of imprisonment while allowing offenders to address the underlying problems. Ultimately, public safety is at stake. Punishment without treatment and rehabilitation results in the release of people who are angrier and less able to contribute to society in a positive way. As David Cayley (1998) has pointed out, prisons are not conducive to rehabilitation.

## A View from the Bench

In a meeting of the Canadian Institute for the Administration of Justice, the Honourable Mr. Justice William Vancise argued that:

> It is clear that imprisonment fails to achieve the objectives of deterrence and rehabilitation in any meaningful way. . . . [It is] an expression of latent vengeance with few positive results. Notwithstanding that failure, there are some offences and some offenders for which imprisonment is the only appropriate penalty because the only way to protect society is by removing the offender from the community. Those crimes which require incarceration are not hard to identify: murder, rape, armed robbery, and those violent crimes where the offender's conduct is so reprehensible that imprisonment is the only alternative to achieve one of the fundamental goals of sentencing—protection of the public.

Source: Canadian Institute for the Administration of Justice 1997

Research from CSC suggests that programs can be effective. Offenders who complete some of the programs described above are less likely to reoffend upon release. Evaluations also suggest that high-risk offenders who receive good treatment are less likely to reoffend, and that treatment is less effective with low-risk offenders (Andrews and Bonta 2006). High-risk offenders who participated in violence prevention programs were almost 30 percent less likely to be returned to custody. Offenders who participated in substance abuse programs were 45 percent less likely to be readmitted to CSC custody. Those who participated in the community maintenance program were almost 30 percent less likely to return to federal custody (Correctional Service of Canada 2009a).

Utilitarian goals aside, our prison system should not undermine the values—such as equality, accountability, efficiency, and justice—discussed in Chapter 2. In Canada we are disproportionately imprisoning Aboriginal people, which violates the principle of equality. In addition, CSC does not regularly or publicly release information on the level of violence in Canadian prisons. The reports cited in this chapter are not, for example, available on their website. Another key question surrounds the cost effectiveness of keeping low-risk offenders in prison rather than in the community. Finally, in relation to ensuring justice, incarceration removes many of the freedoms that are integral to a liberal democracy. To do this in a way that remains just is one of the biggest challenges we face when debating the legitimacy of using prisons to punish or incapacitate. Michal Jackson and Graham Steward, two long-time advocates for prisoners' rights, have written:

> While prison is one of the most difficult environments to respect human dignity, that means we must be ever more vigilant to ensure that the values that we depend on for our quality of life are extended to those in prison. . . . The goal of living in a humane society cannot be surrendered—particularly in our prisons. (Jackson and Stewart 2009)

## Chapter 4

# Community-Based Sentences and Corrections

Although crime is often associated with prison, a large proportion of offenders are serving all or part of their sentences in the community. Thirty percent of admissions to either federal or provincial correctional services are for community corrections and sentences (Calverley 2010). This means that on any given day some 119,965 offenders are being supervised in the community compared to just over 37,000 who are incarcerated.

Community-based sentences include probation and conditional sentences. Conditional sentences are more restrictive than probation, with more close monitoring. The correctional system also supervises offenders in the community who are on parole. Parole allows offenders who have served some time in prison to reintegrate gradually into life outside.

Some new legislation proposes to reduce the use of conditional sentencing and to tighten the eligibility requirements for parole. Prior to the prorogation of Parliament in 2010, Bill C-43 (Strengthening Canada's Corrections System Act) set the stage for a move away from our system of statutory release, which requires offenders to serve the last third of their sentence in the community unless they are deemed likely to commit a serious offence. This follows a recommendation of the CSC Review Panel, which argued that parole should be earned only by offenders who behave while in prison and who participate in and complete correctional programs. Bill C-53, known as Protecting Canadians by Ending Early Release for Criminals Act, proposed the end of accelerated parole, which is an option for non-violent offenders who apply after having served one-sixth of their sentence. A Bill proposed in June 2010, C-39, puts these issues back on the table. Conditional sentences were also targeted in the government's "tough on crime" agenda. Bill C-16 would

# The View from the John Howard Society

John Howard was a famous prison reformer who lived in England in the late eighteenth century. He was outspoken against the inhumane treatment of prisoners and the deplorable conditions of prisons, advocating instead for rehabilitation and reintegration. Today, the John Howard Society of Canada continues this work by advocating for the rights of prisoners and promoting humane and effective responses to crime. They provide support to male offenders both during their incarceration and after their release into the community.

The John Howard Society believes that community-based sentences can and should be imposed on the great majority of offenders. The range of community based sanctions available in Canada is a credit to our country's belief in a rational, principles-based sentencing scheme. The new conditional sentence and the availability of restitution introduced in 1996 offer the courts a wider range of satisfactory options to ensuring offenders have the opportunity to remain in the community making a contribution while accepting the consequences for their behaviour.

Source: John Howard Society of Alberta 1999

have  restricted the use of conditional sentences. Having been elected with a majority government in 2011, the Conservatives have promised to bring these issues back in an omnibus crime bill. This chapter looks at the most recent research; it seems likely that the changes that will be proposed in this bill will have unintended negative consequences.

# Community-Based Sentences

Probation, the most frequently used sentence, is perhaps the most familiar form of community-based sentencing. Almost half of those convicted of a crime in Canada are sentenced to probation. The aim of a probationary sentence is the successful reintegration of the offender into the community. Offenders serving probation live in the community but are required to abide by certain regulations: they must appear before the court on a regular basis, behave well, and notify the court of any changes of address or employment, among other things. Other requirements may include community service, abstaining from alcohol, and attending treatment groups or other types of counselling. Probation can be used on its own or in conjunction with another sanction, such as prison. The sentence, however, must be three years or less to be eligible for probation. Offenders who violate the terms of their probation may be charged and prosecuted, and they may receive jail terms of up to two years.

Probation offers the opportunity for offenders to live relatively normal lives while acquiring help as needed for underlying problems.

Conditional sentences are less common. Parliament introduced this option in 1996 as part of a larger review of sentencing principles and justice policies in Canada. Along with the Principles of Sentencing we saw in Chapter 2, the conditional sentence was part of an effort to change the way we do justice. The goal was to reduce the use of incarceration while providing a sentence that essentially incapacitates the offender. Under conditional sentences, offenders are sentenced to prison but serve their time in the community under severe restrictions, including house arrest and curfews. Section 742 of the Criminal Code outlines the circumstances under which a judge may impose a conditional sentence:

- The offence must be punishable by a maximum term of imprisonment;
- The judge must believe that the offence should receive a term of imprisonment of less than two years;
- The offender must not pose a risk to the community;
- The conditional sentence must achieve the purpose and principles of sentencing (see Chapter 2).

Conditional sentences are designed to ensure that offenders do not reoffend, effectively incapacitating them without actual imprisonment.[1] Offenders who commit certain types of crimes, including terrorism, sexual assault, and some cases of armed robbery, are not eligible to serve conditional sentences. These restrictions are laid out in the Criminal Code.

The Supreme Court of Canada has clarified the difference between conditional sentences and probation: conditional sentences are more punitive and more restrictive than probation. The Court suggested that restrictions for those serving conditional sentences should include house arrest and curfews, and that offenders serving conditional sentences should be aware that breaches of these conditions could result in the remainder of the sentence being served in prison. The Court also stated that a conditional sentence can be longer than the prison sentence that would otherwise have been imposed.[2] Essentially, the Supreme Court has indicated that conditional sentences are, and should be, punitive. They should create hardships for the offender.

Although it may sound counterintuitive, conditional sentences can be seen as a form of imprisonment that is served in the community. To understand this apparent contradiction we must see imprisonment, or incapacitation, as being about restraint and confinement rather than necessarily about institutionalization behind prison walls (Roberts

# A View from the Bench

In commenting on the goals of conditional sentence, Justice William Vancise of the Saskatchewan Court of Appeal has stated that:

> The codified principles of sentencing in [the Criminal Code of Canada] clearly contemplate the importance of offenders accepting responsibility for their actions and acknowledging the harm they cause. The principles are broad enough to permit creativity and to permit the crafting of conditional sentences which can include judicially mandated treatment. Imprisonment is statutorily mandated to be used as a last resort. Conditional sentencing puts the onus on the offender, for example, to comply with a judicially mandated treatment order failing which the offender will be incarcerated. This kind of incentive works.

Source: Canadian Institute for the Administration of Justice 1997

2004a, 40). Offenders are sentenced to a term of imprisonment, and this takes place in the community. Don Davies, Member of Parliament for Vancouver Kingsway, noted that "conditional sentences are not simply a free pass for an offender to have a free vacation in the community" (Davies 2009). In other words, conditional sentences are not an alternative to prison sentences but a replacement for incarceration for some offenders and some offences (Roberts 2004b; Roberts and Gabor 2004).

Julian Roberts, an expert in sentencing trends, sees conditional sentencing as a transformation of our concept of imprisonment as well as an evolution in offender accountability (Roberts 2004b). He suggests that this shift is taking place because people have become frustrated with traditional forms of imprisonment and have turned instead to restorative justice and other more comprehensive responses to crime. For Roberts, conditional sentences ensure that "offenders are confronted on a daily basis, with people aware of their offending, and on whom that offending has had an impact" (Roberts 2004b, 64). He believes that conditional sentences require offenders to participate in solving the problems underlying their criminal activity and to seek the resources required to improve their lives. At the same time, he believes that conditional sentences provide enough surveillance to ensure that offenders will not re-offend while serving their time.

Not all criminologists and criminal justice officials are as enthusiastic. Dawn Moore worries that conditional sentences effectively turn the community into a prison and open up people's private lives to increased government scrutiny, "moving punishment into the private realm of the home and family" (Moore 2007, 340). She argues that the consequence of such a shift may be a worrisome expansion of government power.

The media often portrays conditional sentencing in a negative light. Mike Jenkinson (2005) of the *Edmonton Sun*, for example, complained that house arrest is more like a vacation than a punishment. Mindelle Jacobs (2008) of the *Toronto Sun* similarly described conditional sentences as "where you get to lounge around at home and watch TV for a year." This type of cynicism is common.

Nevertheless, research shows that many Canadians do support conditional sentences. The National Justice Survey (Latimer and Desjardins 2007), for example, found that respondents expressed high levels of support for conditional sentences for non-violent offences, such as small amounts of marijuana possession, car theft, driving under the influence, and break and enter (in the absence of the householder). They were less supportive of conditional sentences in cases of sexual abuse of children, rape at knifepoint, selling a large amount of cocaine, armed robbery, and offences committed while on bail. The respondents resisted giving conditional sentences to repeat violent offenders. Other studies have found a similar opposition to using conditional sentences for serious offences, but these studies also found a preference for conditional sentencing over imprisonment, even in some cases of violence (Latimer and Desjardins 2007).

Respondents are much more open to the use of conditional sentences if they are first fully informed about the options. For example, in one study people were asked to choose between a prison or a conditional sentence for an offender found guilty of break, enter, and theft. One group of the respondents were told only that the offender could receive six months in prison or a six month conditional sentence. Given that choice, only 27 percent chose the conditional sentence. However, when provided with more details about the conditions that would be imposed under the conditional sentence, 64 percent chose that option (Sanders and Roberts 2000). This research suggests that a general reluctance to accept innovative criminal justice responses may have more to do with a lack of information than real concerns about particular policies and programs.

## Parole

Lack of information may also explain why Canadians have little confidence in the parole system. Polls have shown that Canadians have less confidence in the parole system than other sectors, such as policing; in fact, just over half have little or no confidence in the parole system. In another survey, 65 percent of respondents felt that the parole system should be stricter (Stein 2001). The results of this survey are cause for concern, particularly at a time when big changes to the program are being proposed.

Parole, also known as conditional release, is authorized by the Corrections and Conditional Release Act (CCRA). Administration of this program is shared by the Parole Board of Canada and Correctional Service of Canada. The CCRA lays out rules for parole decisions and offender monitoring. Specific decisions on parole are made by the Parole Board, which is informed by information provided from officials with the Correctional Service of Canada. Victims are also included in the process. Once on parole, offenders are supervised by Correctional Service of Canada.

At various points during their sentence, inmates may apply for discretionary releases that must be approved by the Parole Board. Inmates are eligible for day parole either six months after the start of their sentence or six months prior to their eligibility for full parole, whichever date requires them to serve more time in prison. Day parole allows inmates to participate in community-based activities and prepares them for longer periods of release. After serving one-third of their sentence (or after

## The View from a Parolee

The transition from prison to life on the outside is full of challenges. Gayle, who was sentenced to life and served ten years, describes her experience:

I found myself quite paranoid. . . . I didn't feel that I belonged. My son had to remind me to buy new clothes, to change, to get in step with things. I couldn't have cared less because I got used to wearing the same thing every day. . . . Then driving. I found it very strange because the things that I had left behind weren't there. A lot of the buildings were gone and the streets had changed. . . . I had a difficult time in the beginning to find my way around. I'd get turned around very easily. If there was an accident or if I saw a policeman pull somebody over, I would just start shaking. I was terrified of being pulled over and sent back, even though I had no reasons. I wasn't doing anything but I had that great fear. So that part of me, it took me about two years before I felt that I belonged here. Up until then, I didn't feel I belonged. It's a hard thing to describe what I mean by that. I don't really know how to describe it other than I didn't feel safe; I didn't feel a part of this world anymore; I was still inside. In some respects, part of me always will be inside.

Source: Gayle 2008, 104

seven years, whichever is less), most inmates may apply for full parole.[3] Under full parole offenders may serve the remainder of their sentences in the community under CSC supervision. Most also receive support from community-based agencies such as the John Howard Society or the Elizabeth Fry Society.

After serving two-thirds of their sentence, inmates are usually given statutory release. Statutory releases are not discretionary, although the Parole Board may order an offender to be detained if he or she poses a threat to society. All offenders on statutory release are closely monitored by the Parole Board. They are still serving their sentence in the community under the close watch of correctional officials and with certain restrictions on their activities. Those serving life or indeterminate sentences are not subject to statutory release, although those serving life sentences are usually eligible for parole after they have served 25 years. If an inmate is denied parole or statutory release he or she is released into the community at the end of their sentence with no support or supervision.

The practice of statutory release originated in a review of the Parole Act, a piece of legislation that predates the CCRA. Researchers found that low-risk offenders were being released on parole, but that high-risk offenders were being held until the end of their sentences; they were then released into the community with no supervision or help. While it may seem appropriate to keep a high-risk offender in prison as long as possible, research shows that releasing him or her without support is riskier than providing time and support to adjust to life on the outside. Release of high-risk offenders following two-thirds of a term, with support upon release, ultimately enhances public safety.

## Trends in Community-Based Sentences in Canada

Community-based sentences are applied differently to different offender populations. Probation is typical for low-risk offenders. Attending counselling and abstaining from drugs and/or alcohol are the most common conditions of probation. Conditional sentences have been used about equally for property and violent offences. In recent years, judges have used them less often for property offences and more often for drug offences (Roberts 2004b). The number of conditions imposed on offenders is increasing, and becoming more restrictive. For example, a larger proportion of offenders are being supervised under house arrest rather than having restrictions on their movement (Roberts 2002). Judges have increased the punitiveness of conditional sentences, making them an ever more viable way to punish and rehabilitate offenders without requiring actual jail time.

The number of offenders serving probation has been around 100,000 each year for the past 10 years. The proportion of offenders serving probation compared to other sentences has been relatively stable over the years, with about 40 percent serving a term of probation for a violent offence. Typically, terms of probation are between 12 and 18 months (Landry and Sinha 2008). Until recently, the typical length for a conditional sentence was six months, but the length is increasing because judges are using them for a wider range of offences (Roberts and Gabor 2004).

We noted earlier in this chapter that prior to prorogation in 2010, Parliament was considering a bill to limit the use of conditional sentences. If it had passed, the new legislation would have restricted the use of conditional sentences for crimes with a maximum penalty of 14 years or life, and for certain types of serious crimes such as theft over $5,000, auto theft, break and enter, arson, drug trafficking, and crimes involving a weapon. According to Justice Minister Rob Nicholson,

> These amendments show that the government has remained firm in its determination to make sure that those who commit serious crimes serve time behind bars. We want to make it clear that conditional sentences will no longer be available to criminals who commit serious crimes. The government is introducing these amendments in support of our key commitment to take action against crime. (Nicholson 2009)

In a press release, Justice Minister Vic Toews stated that "our new government has made safe streets and communities a key priority. . . . If criminals are to be held to account, they must face a punishment that matches the severity of their crime. . . . People who commit serious crimes should serve their time behind bars, not in the community" (Toews 2006). While the proposed changes seem to fall in line with the public's concern about serious offenders, they do not address the use of conditional sentences for repeat offenders. The government is also promoting the idea that conditional sentences do not adequately punish, and that prison remains the best form of discipline.

## Trends in the Use of Parole in Canada

On a typical day in Canada, almost nine thousand people are under supervision on some form of parole. This number has been increasing.

Just under half of those on parole are on full parole, and 36 percent are on statutory release. Offenders serving full parole are supervised on average for just over two years; the average for statutory release is six months.

The political tide may be shifting away from support for the gradual release of offenders. The CSC Review Panel favoured a system of earned parole, whereby inmates become eligible for parole based on good behaviour and their progress in programs. The Panel suggested that the current system of statutory release discourages offenders from participating in programs to assist with their rehabilitation because they know they will be released after serving only two-thirds of their sentence (Correctional Service of Canada Review Panel 2007). To address these apparent failures, the government has been pursuing changes to the CCRA so that inmates will not be released on parole until they show that they have made progress toward rehabilitation. On the one hand, this seems quite sensible. Inmates who have not addressed the issues that led them to offend are at a higher risk to reoffend. On the other hand, given that most inmates are released eventually, it is unlikely that releasing them "cold," without supervision or opportunity to adjust to the outside, will better protect the public or prevent reoffending.

## Are Community-Based Sentences and Corrections Working?

Chapter 3 examined incapacitation as a central goal of the prison system. Conditional sentences aim to incapacitate but not to institutionalize. As such, they raise questions about whether offenders who pose a risk to society are serving their sentences in the community without adequate supervision.

Offenders have committed serious crimes while serving conditional sentences. However, a look at the comprehensive data available reveals that these cases are anomalies. Most offenders, upwards of 80 percent, complete their conditional sentences without breaching their conditions and without reoffending (Roberts and Gabor 2004). Furthermore, the most common breaches that do occur are of restitution orders and community service work orders (Johnson 2006). Although these breaches can result in criminal charges, they do not constitute threats to public safety. Newly committed criminal offences accounted for only 9 percent of breaches in 2000–2001 (Roberts 2002, 277). Offenders originally sentenced for robbery or break and enter had the highest breach rates, while offenders sentenced for drug-related offences were the least likely (Johnson 2006). The data on completion rates suggest that, despite some anomalous cases, offenders serving conditional sentences do not pose a high level of risk to society. In other words, they are being effectively incapacitated.

Deterrence is another goal of sentencing that can be achieved with conditional sentences. Offenders serving conditional sentences are deterred from committing crimes by the restrictions associated with their sentence (Roberts 2004b). The deterring potential of conditional sentences will depend in large part on the conditions imposed and the amount of supervision and resources available. As Roberts suggests, "the constraints upon the offender have to be real, and the threat of committal to prison must be realistic" (Roberts 2004b, 56). While the conditions being imposed have become more restrictive in recent years, Roberts worries that caseloads of correctional officials are too high to ensure effective supervision (Roberts 2004b, 57). Given that both conditional and community-based sentences are significantly cheaper than institutional incarceration, it seems reasonable to invest some of these savings into better supervision.

These issues of deterrence and incapacitation ultimately lead to a further question: Can probation, conditional sentences, or parole reduce recidivism? Comparatively, it seems that community sentences result in less recidivism than incarceration. According to Statistics Canada, 11 percent of offenders who serve a community sentence become re-involved with corrections after their sentence has ended. This compares to 30 percent of offenders who serve prison sentences and become subsequently involved with corrections (Johnson 2006). An American study also found that offenders who had served a term of house arrest were less likely to be rearrested; and when they were rearrested, their offences tended to be less serious than the offences of those who had served other types of sentences (Ulmer 2001).

It is worth noting, however, that these different recidivism rates could be related to different types of offenders, since those sentenced to incarceration usually have committed more serious crimes than those given community sentences. Still, even though the research in this regard is fairly underdeveloped and we do not have good historical data, there is reason to believe that community sentences can maintain and enhance pro-social relationships (as opposed to the anti-social ones formed while in prison) (Roberts 2004b; Ulmer 2001).

More substantial data is available regarding parole (Parole Board of Canada 2009). Day parole has the highest success rate: over 80 percent are completed without a re-conviction or a breach of conditions. For full parole the figure is about 75 percent. Statutory release has the lowest success rate: 40 percent of offenders on statutory release break the conditions of their parole. Only 2 percent of offenders on statutory release are readmitted to prison for committing a violent crime. To put this in perspective, violent crime committed by those on statutory release between 2006 and 2007 accounted for only 117 incidents (Jackson and Stewart 2009). In 2006, 451,652 violent offences were reported to police making the proportion of violent offences committed by offenders on parole less that 0.03 percent.

However, the above data provide only limited insight into the effect of gradual release on offender recidivism; to see the full picture, we need a broader understanding of its effect on public safety. The CSC Review Panel argued that the reoffending rates of those on statutory release justify tighter restrictions on inmates' eligibility for release. Their report points out that rates of violent offending are three times higher for those on statutory release than on discretionary release, such as day parole. They also point out that most incidents of violence committed by federal offenders are by those on statutory release (Correctional Service of Canada Review Panel 2007). Thus, the conclusion drawn by their report is that statutory release has been a failure. But others interpret the data differently. Jackson and Stewart, for example, argue that eliminating statutory release will increase public safety only if, after its elimination, fewer violent crimes are committed by offenders who previously would have been given a statutory release. These offenders, in other words, would have to be responsible for less than 2 percent of all violent crime, the share of violent crime currently committed by offenders on statutory release (Jackson and Stewart 2009).

The CSC Review Panel also failed to address the fact that inmates who are released from prison at the end of their sentence, having spent no time on parole, are more likely to reoffend than those who have served full parole. Furthermore, the overall rate of parole breaches has been improving in recent years, decreasing by 36 percent between 1996/1997 and 2008/2009 (Parole Board of Canada 2009). Contrary to the recommendations of the CSC Review Panel, these data do not lead to a conclusion that the parole system is really a problem that needs to be fixed. The data could be seen as demonstrating that the parole system is working and is producing increasingly effective results. Furthermore, no research demonstrates that a move to earned parole (the option favoured by the CSC Review Panel) would reduce reoffending. A better interpretation of the numbers is needed before we decide to undertake drastic policy changes to our current system.

Besides arguments about recidivism, common critique of community-based sentences is that they are too lenient. This, however, is a misconception. Many offenders report that conditional sentences are difficult, and the research confirms that they are not the "vacations" that many opponents claim they are. One study of women offenders, for instance, found that being "imprisoned" at home combined the burden of a sentence with the responsibility of running a household (Maidment 2002). Another study of Canadian offenders' responses to community sentencing found that many offenders considered conditional sentences especially difficult because the sentence requires them to actively engage in their reintegration and rehabilitation, unlike a regular prison sentence in which, according to one offender, you just have "to wait it out" (Roberts 2004b, 101).

Another issue to consider is the way in which conditional sentences constrain people's freedom:

> Members of the public tend to take for granted their freedom of movement. If they were to consider the effect of house arrest more carefully they might appreciate that being denied pleasure such as taking one's child to a football match or joining the family on a bank holiday trip to the seaside is real punishment. And unlike a fine or some other sanction, house arrest has social consequences for the offenders. His or her status as an offender is apparent to all other people with whom he or she shares a residence. (Roberts 2004b, 96)

A properly designed and supervised conditional sentence is perhaps more punitive than many may believe.

Victims' groups, however, tend to be more sceptical of community-based sanctions, particularly conditional sentences. Their main objection is that conditional sentences are not harsh enough for any offender who has been convicted of a violent crime (Roberts 2004b, 63). These groups have also raised concerns about offenders serving sentences in the same community as the victim. Mothers against Drunk Driving (MADD) is particularly adamant:

> We are witnessing outrageous conditional sentences relating to violent crimes in our country. It is a travesty of justice that a person who has killed or seriously injured is given the opportunity to avoid the jail-time he or she deserves. Jail time is part of our correctional services in Canada and, especially with the worse types of crimes where there has been a death or serious injury, we need to insist on jail to maintain Canadians' sense of safety and of justice. Common sense dictates that there'd be no conditional sentences for those convicted of any violent crime. (MADD Canada 2004)

Retribution seems to be a clear sentiment in this statement, but is there a blurring of the line between retribution and revenge? This may be an unhelpful approach to policies designed to decrease reoffending.

Community corrections and community-based sentences are not without other criticisms. We might look carefully at how the system of community corrections replicates existing social inequalities. Statistics on Aboriginal offenders, for example, reveal that they are less likely than other racialized groups to be granted full parole. In addition, more restrictions tend to be placed on Aboriginal offenders, and they are more often referred for detention or denied parole by the Parole Board than other offenders. Community corrections must be subject to the same ethics of social justice as other forms of corrections.

Chapter 2 explored accountability as one of the key values of our criminal justice system. Indeed, accountability is central to the policies recommended by the Correctional Service Review Panel. They suggested that the CCRA must ensure a higher level of offender accountability. Reflecting those views, Public Safety Minister Peter Van Loan has argued that statutory release is the "wrong approach," undermining any incentive for inmates to take responsibility for their own actions and participate in programs (Van Loan 2009b). Van Loan argued in a CBC interview that offenders would be held more accountable by ensuring careful adherence to a given correctional plan prior to release on parole (Van Loan 2009a). The conclusion—that such changes will promote more offender accountability—is debatable. Further, it leaves aside any discussion of how the correctional system can be more accountable to the public.

All these values can be assessed in the context of arguments about efficiency. There may be disagreements about retribution and accountability, but clearly effectiveness and cost are equally important issues at stake. The cost for a community sentence is four or five dollars per day; jail is some 20 times more expensive. As the Canadian Criminal Justice Association wrote to the Minister of Public Safety about proposed changes to the system of community corrections:

> While it is fair to debate different approaches to crime, we must always consider what has been shown to work effectively, as well as the costs. No system is perfect and certainly more can be done to raise the rate of successful, safe reintegration back into society. In the meantime however, let us not abandon our knowledge. From a public safety perspective, we should take great care not to undermine a system that has proven itself best able to keep communities relatively safe while returning individuals in a gradual and supervised fashion. (Osler 2010)

## Chapter 5

# Problem-Solving and Specialist Courts

The 1980s saw the development of an innovative new approach to specific offences. Problem-solving and specialist courts are situated within the criminal justice system (and overseen by judges), but their goal is to consider relevant issues that may underlie some criminal behaviour. These courts focus on principles of rehabilitation rather than retribution (Eley 2005). Enhanced judicial oversight and more in-depth case management are key goals; offenders are held accountable but at the same time provided with opportunities to improve their lives.

Problem-solving and specialists courts are expanding across Canada. Drug-treatment and mental-health courts were set up in Toronto in 1998 and have since opened in Vancouver, Edmonton, Regina, Winnipeg, and Ottawa. Mental-health courts are now open in several provinces including Ontario and New Brunswick. The first court specializing in family violence opened in Winnipeg in 1990; several others have opened elsewhere in Canada.

The expansion of these alternative courts has been encouraged by many who welcome the opportunity to address the root causes of crimes associated with drug use or mental illness. In the case of domestic violence, specialized courts provide resources to ensure that the justice system follows through in spite of the relationships between the victim and offender. Court staff have training in the dynamics of specific crimes and particular types of offenders.

Problem-solving and specialist courts have their critics, many of whom question whether they are more effective than traditional courts. How much can drug use or family violence be reduced? Are the treatment programs effective? And a more complex issue arises: Should courts address the social causes of crime or deal with more narrowly just the act of crime itself?

# Drugs

In 2008–9, drug offences constituted only 7 percent of Adult Criminal Court sentences. Almost half of these cases involved possession; the other half involved trafficking. Few of those charged with possession were sentenced to prison, while almost half of those found guilty of trafficking were incarcerated. In 2008–9, just over 4,500 people were admitted to Canadian prisons for drug-related offences. On any given day, 12 percent of the federal inmate population and 8 percent of those sentenced to provincial custody are serving time for a drug offence (Calverley 2010). Drug crimes constitute a fairly small proportion of court cases, and drug offenders similarly make up a small proportion of those held in Canadian jails.

According to police data, the rate of drug offences has been increasing since the mid-1990s (Dauvergne 2009). However, we have no way of knowing whether the increase is due to a real change in people's behaviour or changes in policing or legislation.[1] In 2007, police reported 100,000 drug-related incidents. Cannabis was involved in 62 percent of these and 75 percent involved possession. Cocaine-related cases constituted one-quarter of drug offences known to police. Less than 1 percent of incidents were related to heroin. This means that in 2007, police dealt with just over 62,000 incidents involving marijuana, just under 23,000 cases involving cocaine, and almost 800 cases involving heroin. This represents a very small proportion of the more than two million crimes that police deal with each year.

# Drug-Treatment Courts

Drug-treatment courts emerged in the late 1980s in the United States in response to the increasing incarceration of drug addicts whose crimes were related to addiction. Drug courts are now the most common type of problem-solving court (Werb and Kerr 2007). Several countries have professional associations for those working in drug courts, and the United Nations has identified principles for their operation[2]; drug-treatment courts have even been described as a "movement" within the criminal justice system (Wilson, Mitchell, and Mackenzie 2006).

The first drug-treatment court in Canada was established in Toronto in 1998 as a way of diverting addicted offenders away from jail. Since then, these courts have emerged in several Canadian cities, often in response to a localized drug problem and dealing mainly with non-violent drug-related offences. The court in Vancouver, for example, targets injection-drug users mainly in the Downtown Eastside.

The hope is that drug-treatment courts will halt the revolving door of drug-addicted offenders in the criminal justice system, as well as reduce the social and economic costs of drug abuse. One judge states that "public interest is best served by a situation where an individual manages to overcome an addiction and no longer needs to finance this addiction; then the cycle is broken" (United Nations Office on Drugs and Crime 2011). Dawn Moore, a Canadian researcher, has noted the same theme emerging out of her observations in the Toronto drug-treatment court (Moore 2007).

Drug courts typically include two main components: treatment and intensive supervision. Treatment of addictions is mandatory for offenders participating in drug-treatment court. The court may order various programs, based on a treatment plan that includes group, individual, or family counselling. Some participants may be required to attend a residential treatment program, but most are treated on an outpatient basis. The court supervises offenders through the types of restrictions usually applied to those on probation. In addition, participants may be required to submit to random drug testing. The assumption is that treating offenders' addictions will reduce their motivation to reoffend (La Prairie et al. 2002; Slinger and Roesch 2010).

Participant compliance is the key, and hence courts offer various incentives and rewards to encourage participants. Gift cards, usually for local coffee shops, are a typical reward for compliance. The courts may also impose sanctions when participants fail to comply with treatment plans or if they test positive for drug use. Remand is commonly used as a consequence for those who do not follow through on their treatment plans. In Winnipeg, judges may impose additional restrictions (such as curfews) and more frequent drug testing. Non-compliant participants may be sent back to the regular court system. A participant who completes a treatment plan and complies with the other restrictions "graduates" from drug-treatment court; charges against them may be dropped (Slinger and Roesch 2010).

## Criminal Justice and Mental Illness

Mental health is a major issue in Canada. Health Canada estimates that 20 percent of Canadians will experience a mental illness at some time in their lives and that more than 8 percent will experience a bout of major depression (Health Canada 2002). A survey of Canadians found that 4

# The View from a Mental-Health Court Judge

Judge Al Brien is a provincial court judge in New Brunswick working in the mental-health courts in Saint John.

> With the closure of public psychiatric hospitals and the lack of adequate funding for resources to help the mentally ill cope in the community, jails became the alternative psychiatric institutions. Provincial courts had experienced a steady increase of people often displaying difficult behaviour in the courtroom and repeat offenses were all too common. The time constraints of a busy docket precluded any in-depth analysis of these cases and any disposition of therapeutic justice. (Brien 2004, 50)

percent reported having experienced the symptoms of major depression in the past 12 months but that only one-third had sought treatment (Statistics Canada 2004). In the past decade, research alongside advocacy has helped uncover the full extent of mental illness.

Chapter 3 considered how inmates in Canadian prisons suffer disproportionately from mental illnesses. Research from Correctional Service of Canada suggests that 12 percent of the federal inmate population displays symptoms of some form of mental illness. This number has almost doubled over the past 10 years. Furthermore, caseloads have increased for the provincial Review Boards that oversee people who have been deemed unfit to stand trial or found not criminally responsible for their crime due to mental illness or disability (Schneider, Bloom, and Heerema 2007). As the crime rate has decreased, the proportion of offenders with mental illnesses has increased.

Many critics argue that cuts made to mental health services during the 1990s lie at the root of the problem (Schneider, Bloom, and Heerema 2007). These cuts resulted in fewer psychiatric hospitals across the country; as a consequence many people suffering from poor mental health became "patients of the criminal justice system" (Schneider, Bloom, and Heerema 2007, 26). Now many mentally ill Canadians who have committed minor offences are repeatedly appearing in Canadian courts (Schneider, Bloom, and Heerema 2007).

## Mental-Health Courts

Mental-health courts focus on diverting mentally ill offenders from the criminal justice system and providing treatment. On its website, the

Toronto Mental Health Court—one of the most comprehensive courts of its kind in the world—describes its goal as "decriminalizing the mentally ill."[3] Along with drug courts, mental-health courts are aimed at reducing the "revolving door" of offenders who continue to offend, partly because the traditional criminal justice system fails to address the root cause of their troubles.

Mental-health courts improve service to offenders with mental illnesses in two key respects. First, they provide quicker access to pre-trial mental health assessments. Research from the Toronto court suggests that it has been effective in speeding up client access to services. More timely access to assessment leads to faster treatment of mental illness, and this ultimately leads to better outcomes for offenders. Mental-health courts also improve service by incorporating diverse professionals into a collaborative team that includes judges, dedicated Crown and defence lawyers, social workers, and psychiatrists. These teams are better able to meet the diverse needs of the mentally ill than are traditional court staff.

Mental-health court processes vary, but typically an accused person must have been diagnosed with a mental illness or intellectual disability prior to admission. Judges usually also consider other factors, including public safety and the connection, if any, between the offence and the mental illness. Clients are offered an individualized treatment plan, to which they must agree. They must also report to court officials at regular intervals. Those who fail to comply may be removed from the program. Upon successful completion, charges may be withdrawn or non-custodial sentences imposed, depending on the nature of the crime, public safety considerations, and the availability of community support.

## Domestic Violence

Beginning in the 1990s, the issue of family violence came to the attention of activists, politicians, and the general public. We now know that many violent crimes are committed by individuals who are known to and intimate with the victims. In 2007, for example, 23 percent of violent crimes reported to the police had been committed by a family member. Twelve percent of all violent crimes involved domestic violence—in other words, violence perpetuated by a current spouse, common-law partner, or ex-spouse (Taylor-Butts 2008).

In the 1980s and 1990s, feminist activists and academics voiced concerns that the criminal justice system was failing to confront domestic violence. Men accused of assaulting their partners were not being arrested. In instances where police did lay charges, the cases often fell apart because prosecutors were reluctant to proceed or victims did

# The View from K Court

K Court refers to the specialized domestic-violence court operating in downtown Toronto. In describing the work of the Crown Attorney in this court, one representative has said:

> They don't do any other cases so they have the time to properly prepare. They all do the assessment. They can't meet with all the victim witnesses ahead of time and one Crown has carriage of the file so if there's disclosure of problems, then they've identified matters for discussing with defence ahead of time and what the outstanding issues are going to be at trial. (Eley 2005, 118)

not want to testify. And when abusive men were sentenced, very often the sentences were inappropriately lenient. The criminal justice system was not adequately protecting victims (Tutty, Ursel, and Douglas 2008) and the crime was not being denounced.

Criminal justice agencies responded to the complaints with tough "zero tolerance" policies. Police forces across Canada introduced mandatory or pro-arrest policies, designed to ensure that police officers took complaints of domestic violence seriously and laid charges when circumstances warranted. Prosecutors adopted similar policies—pushing charges through to court even if victims recanted their testimony. Domestic-violence courts emerged out of these efforts.

Domestic-violence courts are generally considered to be "specialized" courts rather than problem-solving courts. Officials working in these courts specialize in the dynamics and complexities associated with domestic violence. The relationship between the victim and the offender distinguishes these often difficult and complex cases. Victim safety, for example, is a major concern that can be overlooked by the regular court system. Specialist knowledge, training, and procedures help ensure offender accountability and victim safety.

To work effectively, specialized domestic-violence courts have to balance three underlying principles: "(1) early intervention for low-risk offenders; (2) vigorous prosecution for serious and/or repeat offenders; and (3) a commitment to rehabilitation and treatment" (Tutty, Ursel, and Douglas 2008, 76). Courts across the country balance these principles differently. The Toronto court, for example, places a higher premium on convictions than some others. It provides a coordinated prosecution model to help ensure victim cooperation (Dawson and Dinovitzer 2008; Eley 2005). Other courts, such as HomeFront in Calgary, focus more on treatment. Charges may be dropped if a man successfully completes the court-ordered treatment program (Tutty, Ursel, and Douglas 2008). Here, the goal is for swift intervention and treatment to prevent some men from becoming chronic offenders (Tutty, McNichol, and Christensen 2008).

# Evaluating Problem-Solving and Specialist Courts

Problem-solving and specialist courts may both denounce and deter particular crimes. Denunciation is a particularly important goal for domestic-violence courts, given past failures of the justice system to address domestic violence as a crime. In recent years, we have seen harsher sentences, increased conviction rates, and fewer cases dropped (Hornick et al. 2008; Tutty, McNichol, and Christensen 2008; Tutty, Ursel, and Douglas 2008; Ursel and Hagyard 2008). Deterrence is a goal for drug-treatment and mental-health courts. Offenders may comply with conditions imposed by the court in order to avoid the potentially harsher punishment they may receive in the regular court stream. They may continue with treatment because of the threat of being sent back to the regular court system.

Rehabilitation is the main goal of drug-treatment and mental-health courts. Judging from their respective completion rates, rehabilitation efforts are more successful in mental-health courts than in drug courts. For example, the mental-health court in Saint John, New Brunswick, reported that between 2000 and 2004 just over three-quarters of those admitted to the program successfully completed it. In comparison, while some drug-treatment courts have better success rates than others, research has shown that only half the participants complete the programs (Belenko 1998; Latimer, Morton-Bourgon, and Crétien 2006). In Vancouver, 14 percent completed the court's drug-treatment program (Public Safety Canada 2009a); in Toronto, the number was 16 percent (Public Safety Canada 2008). As a result of these high drop-out rates, we cannot draw solid conclusions about the success of these courts.

The rehabilitative success of drug-treatment courts can also be measured by evaluating participants' subsequent drug use. Data from the Vancouver court shows that 30 percent of those who successfully completed the program tested positive for drug use within six months of completing the program (Public Safety Canada 2009a). Furthermore, almost all participants tested positive six months after their participation ended. These numbers suggest that the treatment programs are effective only for a very small proportion of people initially admitted to the court. With the data we have thus far it seems that very few participants stop using drugs as a result of participating in drug-treatment court. As will be discussed in the next chapter, the lack of success in this regard may be due to the disconnect between treatment programs that expect abstinence and the lived realities for people suffering from addictions.

Reduced recidivism is often used as an indicator of the effectiveness of rehabilitation. However, the quality and scope of research on recidivism rates associated with different types of problem-solving courts vary considerably (Slinger and Roesch 2010). Only drug-treatment courts have been submitted to random control trials—the most rigorous test of whether an intervention is effective.[4] In a trial, researchers compare the outcomes among those who were randomly chosen to participate in drug-treatment courts with those who were not. These studies, in the US and Australia, have produced mixed results (Gottfredson and Exum 2002; Lind et al. 2002; Turner et al. 2002). Evaluations of courts in Canada, using less rigorous research methods, have produced similarly mixed results (Public Safety Canada 2008; Public Safety Canada 2009a; Werb and Kerr 2007). Given the strength of the research design in these studies we cannot make any conclusions about whether drug-treatment courts reduce recidivism.

Mental health and domestic-violence courts have not been subjected to the same style of rigorous evaluation as drug-treatment courts. One comprehensive research project in the US found reductions in recidivism among clients of mental-health courts (Cosden et al. 2003). The court in Saint John, New Brunswick, also reports good outcomes in this regard. Research on domestic-violence courts similarly suggests that reoffending is reduced among men who complete court-ordered treatment (Hoffart and Clarke 2004). But this literature does not, however, include any random trials or experimental research. In other words, in the absence of further research, making properly informed policy decisions is limited.

Chapter 2 discussed how utilitarian goals such as deterrence and rehabilitation do not take into account either the principle of retribution or questions about the fair distribution of punishment. To be properly retributive, courts must sentence similar crimes, committed in similar circumstances, consistently. One motivation for the development of domestic courts was a desire to see more punitive sentencing in cases of domestic violence. By tracking and comparing sentencing patterns, these courts are well placed to ensure retribution. We could also see drug-treatment and mental-health courts in terms of retribution, with the difference that they promote lighter sentences. The assumption is that harsh punishment is a disproportionate response under certain circumstances. While these courts do not adopt the "tough on crime"

# The View from a Critic

Judge Morris Hoffman of the Second Judicial District Court of Denver, Colorado, is an outspoken critic of drug-treatment courts: "We have rushed headlong into them [drug courts]—driven by politics, judicial pop psychopharmacology, fuzzy-headed notions about 'restorative justice' and 'therapeutic jurisprudence,' and by the bureaucrats' universal fear of being the last on the block to have the latest administrative gimmick" (Hoffman 2001, 1444).

rhetoric of some retributionists, they do emphasize the proportionality principle articulated in the Principles of Sentencing.

Chapter 2 also raised questions about the social values reflected in our different responses to crime. Justice was one of the values highlighted. On the one hand, problem-solving courts offer a "Cadillac" model of justice by providing participants with fast-track access to treatment and social services (Moore 2007; 2009). Justice may also be better served for society at large by addressing the underlying causes of offending. On the other hand, some critics argue that court-ordered mandatory treatment programs are coercive and ignore social structural issues, such as poverty (Moore 2009). Offenders know that by refusing treatment they will face potentially harsher punishment. In some drug-treatment courts, participants must waive some of the rights, including the right to plead not guilty (Moore 2007). These processes may undermine the due process safeguards critical to ensuring that justice is fair (Berman and Feinblatt 2001).

Similar questions have been raised about the pro-prosecution stance of most domestic-violence courts. The concern here is about justice for the victims rather than the offenders. The policies applied in domestic-violence courts "emphasize arrest and punishment of offenders over meeting the needs of victims" (Johnson 2010). However, this argument does not account for the concerns of women who do not want their partners to go to jail—indeed, many need their partners' financial support. Under these circumstances, incarceration may have unintended consequences.

A final issue with problem-solving and specialist courts is efficiency. Only drug-treatment courts have been assessed from this angle. In the US, these courts are viewed as a cost-effective response to drug-related crimes. Less expensive than jail and law enforcement, they also save the costs of pre-trial detention (Belenko 1998).

These arguments may not, however, apply to the Canadian situation. Sentences for drug offences are much less harsh and therefore less costly in Canada. Furthermore, conditional sentences can be used in many cases involving drug offences (La Prairie et al. 2002). Assessments in Canada also suggest that it costs more to put an offender through drug-treatment court than regular court (Werb and Kerr 2007). The high drop-out rate described earlier further confounds our ability to determine the efficacy of these courts. More research will be required before we can draw any conclusions about cost effectiveness.

As problem-solving and specialized courts become more common across the country, questions about their effectiveness as well as how well they reflect our social values abound. We might also ask whether the criminal justice system should become the "preferred gateway to the treatment system" (Anderson 2001, 473). Relying on referrals from the justice system could undermine the voluntary treatment system. Questionable too is the notion that we wait until an individual has committed a crime before investing in treatment:

> The lurking question then is why wait until an individual has been hyper criminalized to provide him with extensive social services? That is, if we recognize that ultimately people need stable housing, health care, someone to talk to, employment, and education, then why wait until they are facing their fourth or fifth go round with the justice system to offer them intensive support? This is less a critique of the [drug-treatment courts] than it is an attempt to remain vigilant to the much deeper needs of people who eventually do end up in conflict with the law. Perhaps the reasons why drug-treatment courts have questionable success rates is that they are, in effect, closing the barn door after the horse has run. (Moore 2009)

It may indeed be that access to viable, voluntary treatment programs is the real solution (Anderson 2001).

## Chapter 6

# Harm Reduction and Crime Prevention

We saw above that problem-solving courts raise questions about poor access to treatment. This chapter considers two approaches to crime that bypass the traditional criminal justice system and shift our thinking away from criminalization and the criminal justice system. Crime-prevention programs and policies treat crime as a preventable social problem. Programs and policies address the needs of high-risk populations or geographical areas. Harm reduction is more narrowly focused on problems associated with substance use and abuse, treating drug use as a health problem rather than a legal one. Programs range from public education campaigns against drunk driving to needle exchange systems for inmates.

Governments across Canada have embraced crime prevention but remain more ambivalent, and sometimes opposed to, harm reduction. The federal government has committed $63 million annually to crime prevention programs. We are among the 21 other countries in the world with a crime prevention strategy and a national agency to coordinate the implementation of the strategy (International Centre for the Prevention of Crime 2010). By contrast, harm-reduction receives less support, especially when it comes to programs for intravenous drug users. Across the country, access to harm reduction programs in jails and prisons varies widely. Furthermore, the federal government is fighting one of the most innovative programs—the drug injection site in Vancouver.

# Crime Prevention

Broadly speaking, crime prevention involves any activity that potentially reduces crime. The International Centre for the Prevention of Crime (2010, 1) cites a UN definition of crime prevention as:

> strategies and measures that seek to reduce the risk of crimes occurring, and their potential harmful effects on individuals and society, including fear of crime, by intervening to influence their multiple causes.

This definition focuses on the outcome rather than the content of any program or policy. Crime prevention activities are often undertaken by agencies outside the criminal justice system—a municipality may invest in better lighting in public parks in an effort to reduce vandalism; a province may promote a school-based anti-bullying program; a community may initiate a mentoring program for youth at risk of gang involvement. Because they are proactive crime prevention, such programs are neither hard nor soft on crime (Sherman et al. 1998).

Stephen Schneider (2009) provides a detailed contrast between traditional criminal justice and crime prevention. He describes crime prevention as proactive rather than reactive. He also emphasizes that crime prevention is more flexible than traditional responses to crime, given that policies and programs are developed to match the particular needs of a community or population. In theory, crime prevention programs should be developed at the community—rather than government—level. In practice, programs tend to be funded by the state but governed by citizens. These characteristics make crime prevention an attractive alternative to the traditional criminal justice response.

The United Nations has outlined several different approaches to crime prevention (International Centre for the Prevention of Crime 2010, 2). Crime prevention through social development (CPTSD) assumes that crime is caused by:

> a combination of social environmental risk factors (e.g., poverty, poor role models, parental neglect or abuse, inadequate schooling etc.) and personal risk factors (e.g., behavioural, psychological and cognitive problems. (Schneider 2009, 77)

Programs and policies focus both on prevention of offending and victimization and tend to work among and address the needs of vulnerable or at-risk populations. The development of community recreation centres or adult basic education programs are examples of programs that aim to prevent crime through social development. A different approach to crime prevention includes changes in the physical or built environment. Known as situational crime prevention, the goal is to reduce the opportunities for offending, increase the effort needed to offend and increase the risk of being caught. Lighting in a public park and neighbourhood watch programs are examples. Finally, some crime prevention programs target people who have already offended and aim to help reintegrate them into the community and prevent them from reoffending.

In Canada crime prevention efforts at the federal level are guided by the National Crime Prevention Strategy. The strategy currently targets children and youth, high-risk offenders, and Aboriginal and northern communities with high crime rates.[1] On their website, the National Crime Prevention Centre (NCPC) states that it aims to "[p]rovide national leadership on effective and cost-efficient ways to both prevent and reduce crime by addressing known risk factors in high-risk populations and places."[2]

The Centre funds projects that aim to prevent crime. The NCPC has also developed resources for community groups to aid in the development and evaluation of crime prevention programs based on the best practices emerging in the literature. This work speaks to a secondary goal of the NCPC, to develop a body of research that supports the development of effective interventions.[3]

## The View from the Canadian Council on Social Development

The Canadian Council on Social Development is a not-for-profit organization that works to promote progressive social policies. They advocate CPTSD.

Social conditions such as housing, family income, and education leave their deepest marks on children and youth. Improvement in these social conditions has been shown to open up new vistas for young people who might otherwise end up behind bars.

This is the principle behind crime prevention through social development (CPTSD): promoting well-being through social, health, and educational measures. Such international authorities as the United Nations (2002) argue that CPTSD is effective, particularly with children and youth.

By investing in kids to provide them with positive life experiences, we can avoid the considerable harms and costs of crime and victimization.

Source: Canadian Council on Social Development n.d.

The NCPC is guided by the National Crime Prevention Strategy. The Strategy assumes that crime can be reduced or prevented by targeting the risk factors associated with criminal offending. These risk factors exist at various levels including individual, family, peer, school, and community. Individual-level factors include behavioural problems and early use of drugs and alcohol. Family-related risks increase when parents or other family members are involved with crime or when there is violence in the family. Similarly, people with crime-involved or violent peers are at more risk. At the community level, the availability of drugs, guns, and a lack of social cohesion are related with higher crime rates. Programs funded by the NCPC often target more than one of these factors, aiming to reduce their impact (National Crime Prevention Centre 2009).

Crime prevention has many advocates, particularly in government and criminal justice-related agencies. Social agencies are also starting to see it as a positive development, especially with the increasing interest in CPTSD. While many academics promote crime prevention, others have raised concerns. Kevin Haggerty questions why social programs such as adult basic education, family planning, and after-school recreation are presented as crime prevention strategies. He suggests that such programs are "the type of things that should be done in a just and compassionate society," regardless of whether they reduce crime (Haggerty 2008, 119). Others have questioned the focus on risk management in crime prevention (Hughes 1998) and the lack of focus on women's safety issues (Shaw and Andrew 2005).

## Harm Reduction

By targeting risk factors, crime prevention policies and programs aim to stop crime before it happens. Harm-reduction programs focus on substance use and abuse, dealing broadly with a wide range of drugs, not only with those that are criminalized in the Controlled Drug and Substances Act. Rather than preventing drug use, harm reduction targets the negative effects of drugs. Like crime prevention, harm reduction shifts our response away from the justice system; it goes even further, however, questioning whether criminalization strategies should be our only response to drug abuse and use.

Harm reduction addresses the negative effect of drugs without the expectation that users will cease using. The goal is to reduce the tangible harms caused by substance use. The Centre for Addiction and Mental Health (CAMH) adopts the following definition: "any program or policy designed to reduce drug-related harm without requiring the cessation of drug use" (Centre for Addiction and Mental Health 2002, 3). The approach lies in stark contrast to zero-tolerance policies that impose punishment and stigmatize users.

Harm reduction takes a holistic approach to harms that can exist at the individual, community, or social level. As an example, a needle-exchange program for intravenous drugs reduces the dangers associated with needle sharing; prohibiting smoking in public places reduces the harm associated with second-hand smoke.

When dealing with illegal drug use, harm reduction is sometimes part of a larger strategy. Vancouver exemplifies a comprehensive response in its "four pillars" approach:

## Prevention

Promoting healthy families and communities, protecting child and youth development, preventing or delaying the start of substance use among young people, and reducing harm associated with substance use. Successful prevention efforts aim to improve the health of the general population and reduce differences in health between groups of people.

## The View from the Centre for Addictions and Mental Health

The Canadian Association of Mental Health advocates for harm reduction and more regulation, rather than criminalization, of substances that create threats to public safety. They do not argue for the decriminalization of drugs; rather, the goal is for our response to addictions to recognize "a balance between control and compassion" (Centre for Addiction and Mental Health 2002, 3). They argue:

> In public health, laws are not moral absolutes, but are instruments that are used to set standards and achieve health objectives for individuals, communities and society. In deciding between criminal and regulatory law, a harm reduction stance asks for proof of what policy components are most effective for reducing specific drug-related harms. Punitive sanctions would then be reserved for those drug use behaviours that pose a threat to the safety or well being of others, such as smoking in offices, selling to minors or providing a contaminated product. Public health regulation generally provides more flexibility than criminal law in fitting the solution to the problem.

Source: Centre for Addiction and Mental Health n.d.

### Treatment

Offering individuals access to services that help people come to terms with problem substance use and lead healthier lives, including outpatient and peer-based counselling, methadone programs, daytime and residential treatment, housing support, and ongoing medical care.

### Harm reduction

Reducing the spread of deadly communicable diseases, preventing drug overdose deaths, increasing substance users' contact with health care services and drug treatment programs, and reducing consumption of drugs in the street.

### Enforcement

Recognizing the need for peace and quiet, public order and safety in the Downtown Eastside and other Vancouver neighbourhoods by targeting organized crime, drug dealing, drug houses, problem businesses involved in the drug trade, and improving coordination with health services and other agencies that link drug users to withdrawal management (detox), treatment, counselling [sic] and prevention services.

Source: City of Vancouver 2008

Not everyone agrees that drug-related policies should include all four pillars. Some commentators argue that harm reduction should not be part of a strategy that involves enforcement (Hathaway and Tousaw 2008). They suggest that advocates of harm reduction would be more consistent with the underlying premise of harm reduction if they clearly advocated for the decriminalization of drugs. The argument is that as long as drugs remain illegal, the harm created by the black market and the legal stigma can never be eliminated.

Harm-reduction programs are important because criminalization and zero tolerance strategies have had a limited effect. In the US, the war on drugs has led to an unmanageable number of people in jail. Chapter 3 discussed efforts at controlling prisoners' access to drugs, which have had little effect. CAMH concludes, "most criminal justice based interventions against illicit drug use are costly, have no supporting evidence of effectiveness and can be shown to augment harm to health and social functioning" (Centre for Addiction and Mental Health 2002, 3).

Whether we believe that drug use is acceptable or not, it seems certain that for heavy users or those suffering with addictions criminalization only exacerbates their problems.

We should also consider harm reduction in light of problems we discussed in earlier chapters. Chapter 6 revealed that most people who go through drug courts do not complete treatment programs. Chapter 3 described the negative effects of drug use in Canadian prisons. Almost three-quarters of inmates in federal custody are assessed as having some form of substance abuse problem. On top of this, almost one-quarter of inmates have severe substance abuse problems, in contrast to 3 percent of the Canadian population (Statistics Canada 2003). A comparison of drug type is also striking. The Canadian Addiction Survey (Adlaf, Begin, and Sawka 2005) found that roughly half of those Canadians who responded admitted to using marijuana at some point in their life. Fourteen percent reported using it within the past year. In contrast, 40 percent of inmates reported having used marijuana in the six months prior to their arrest (Correctional Service of Canada n.d.). Rates of heroin and cocaine use also vary significantly. Twenty-three percent of federal inmates admitted using cocaine or other stimulants in the six months prior to arrest (Correctional Service of Canada n.d.). This compares to only about 10 percent of the general population who have ever used

# The View from the British Columbia Lower Mainland

Intravenous drug-use on the lower mainland has been an issue for at least the past two decades. In a report commissioned by the Medical Health Officers of the Lower Mainland, based on interviews with drug users, the Lower Mainland Working Group on Communicable Diseases concluded that:

> Much of the treatment available in the Lower Mainland is based on an abstinence model, and many programs follow a 12-step approach to recovery. Many injection drug users find these models alienating and non-supportive, and are unable to reach or maintain recovery with them. We spoke with numerous IDUs [intravenous drug users] who had been in and out of detox scores of times, who had endured treatment models which reinforced perceptions of self-negativity and failure while preventing them from addressing their core addiction issues. Despite these barriers, many wanted to end their addiction so strongly that they kept returning for treatment. There is a need for addiction treatment models tailored specifically to the needs of injection drug users.

Source: Bognar, Legare, and Ross 1998, 16

these drugs (Adlaf, Begin, and Sawka 2005). It is clear from these numbers that prisons, in particular, must respond adequately to an inmate population suffering from drug issues.

Despite the many failures of the criminal justice system's response to drug problems, the Canadian government has been moving away from harm reduction in recent years. The federal government's policy to tackle drug use, the Anti-Drug Strategy, does not reference harm reduction as one of its goals.[4] It focuses exclusively on treatment, prevention, and enforcement, including tougher penalties. When it was introduced in 2007, the government presented it as a get-tough policy that explicitly rejected harm reduction. Stephen Harper was quoted as saying that harm reduction is not part of the drug policy: "Because if you remain a drug addict, I don't care how much harm you reduce, you're going to have a short and miserable life" (Canadian Press 2007).

The trend away from harm reduction was also evidenced in the CSC Review Panel. While CSC policy on drug use and transmission of infectious diseases is explicitly premised on a harm reduction approach, the CSC Review Panel has encouraged a move away from harm reduction. Like the Anti-Drug Strategy, the panel emphasized enforcement and zero tolerance (Correctional Service of Canada Review Panel 2007).[5] This advice goes against what CSC's own research tells us about the positive effect of harm-reduction policies in prisons as well as the advice of many national and international medical and criminal justice associations.[6]

# The View from a Critic

For people who view drugs as a criminal rather than a health issue, safe injection sites are the wrong approach. In "Safe Injection Sites Don't Make Sense," Guy Bennett argues that:

> There are 12,000 heroin addicts currently living in British Columbia. Heroin is illegal in this country. So they are all, by definition, criminals. To maintain law and order, it's imperative that we treat our criminals like criminals.
>
> Failure to do so demoralizes the law-abiding masses, and causes the criminals themselves to lose respect for us. Criminals want to be captured and punished. That's why they're criminals. When addicts inject heroin publicly (as many of them are doing now) they are screaming for intervention. The only decent response is to arrest them, detox them—and sentence them to lengthy terms of hard labour.

Source: Bennett cited in Boyd, MacPherson, and Osborn 2009, 109

In contrast to the trend in the federal government, provinces and municipalities are implementing community-based harm-reduction programs. In terms of opiate drug use, many cities have needle exchange programs: there are more than two hundred such programs operating across Canada. Methadone is also widely available as a substitution for those with opiate addictions. Vancouver has a safe injection site where intravenous drug users can go to use clean equipment and inject in a safe environment. Montreal is considering the development of a similar agency. The federal government opposes the development of safe injection sites but recently lost a Supreme Court challenge of the legality of the site in Vancouver.

## Evaluating Crime Prevention and Harm Reduction

Earlier chapters evaluated responses to crime by assessing how well they achieved utilitarian goals such as deterrence, incapacitation, or rehabilitation. Using these concepts, what conclusions can be drawn about crime prevention and harm reduction?

Research on crime prevention finds equivocal results. In one large review, researchers found that just over one-third of the programs were either effective or promising. Sixteen percent were ineffective. In just under half the programs the researchers could not assess effectiveness (Sherman et al. 2002). The projects in this review were diverse and spread over a large geographic area. They were also developed in the absence of a body of research to guide their work.

Yet emerging research is showing some patterns around which programs are effective. For example, parent training programs do not appear to be very effective, but working with at-risk children can be (Welsh and Farrington 2005). Research also suggests that programs involving parents and children show promise. Teaching children social skills can provide them with the capacity to stay away from involvement with crime. Some programs that target offenders are effective, especially those that provide drug treatment and cognitive behavioural therapy. On the other hand, programs such as boot camps and so-called "scared straight" programs, which involve tours of prisons for at-risk youth, do not work (Welsh and Farrington 2005).

Some crime prevention programs target geographic areas rather than individuals, and have been shown to reduce the crime rates in these areas. For example, "hot spots" policing, where police focus their patrols in certain areas looks promising (Welsh and Farrington 2005). Other experiments in changing patrols or enhancing the visibility of police have found these changes do not effectively reduce crime, although they do improve relations between the police and the public (Champion 2007). The use of video cameras and lighting also seems to reduce crime in particular areas, but we do not know if crime has merely been displaced elsewhere (Welsh and Farrington 2005).

The growing body of research on harm-reduction programs is more unequivocal, suggesting that they do reduce the harm associated with substance use. Public Health Canada has completed a comprehensive review of needle-distribution programs in prisons around the world (Public Health Agency of Canada 2006). They found that needle-distribution programs reduced the level of needle sharing and the number of overdoses, as well as other health issues such as skin infection. Research also suggests that clean needle programs provide addicts with more opportunities to come into treatment programs of their own accord, when ready.

This point has been reflected in the experience of Insite, the safe injection site in Vancouver. The evaluations of the agency show that it benefits both the individuals who use the site and the community more generally.[7] Benefits for individuals include an increased likelihood of seeking treatment; clients who used the clinic weekly or more were 1.7 times more likely to seek treatment than those who visited less often (Kerr et al. 2006). People using Insite are also less likely to share needles (Kerr et al. 2005). In the community more generally, a recent study published in a major medical journal reports that overdose deaths decreased by 35 percent in a 500-metre radius of the clinic. This compares to a decrease of 9 percent in Vancouver as a whole (Marshall et al. 2011). One large evaluation found fewer instances of public drug injection and fewer needles discarded in the streets (Kerr et al. 2006). These positive findings are further supported by research showing that the safe-injection site does not appear to have unintended consequences such as increased drug use in the area (Kerr et al. 2006; Kerr et al. 2007).

Concrete outcomes aside, both crime prevention and harm reduction espouse values that contrast with a more traditional approach. It is possible to argue that many crime prevention programs are part of our more general obligation to ensure a just and equitable society. Likewise, commentators have suggested that harm-reduction programs are a matter of rights, especially for prisoners (Chu and Elliott 2009; Kerr et al. 2004). The argument is that governments bear the responsibility to protect inmates from harm. The legislation guiding CSC policies, the Corrections and Conditional Release Act, confirms that prisoners retain the same rights as those not imprisoned. The only rights they lose are those explicitly removed or restricted as part of the sentence. The Conditional

Release Act also states that the medical care in prison will be the same as that in the community. Justice, then, cannot be achieved if the state denies these rights to inmates.

Both crime prevention and harm reduction are premised on values that promote social justice. The underlying logic differs from that of traditional criminal justice policies. Politically, crime prevention is more palatable and, as a result, is better funded. Harm reduction, especially when associated with intravenous drug users, raises alarm among some levels of government, despite clear evidence of its effectiveness.

## Chapter 7

# Restorative Justice

In 1974, two teenagers in Elmira, Ontario, vandalized several properties in their community. Russell Kelly, one of the young people involved, describes how he and a friend went on a rampage. They slashed the tires on 24 cars. They also threw rocks into homes and vandalized businesses and street signs. They damaged 22 properties in the early hours of the morning. At the end, he states that: "[w]hen we had enough of this craziness we headed back to the apartment and passed-out" (Kelly n.d.).[1]

The youths were apprehended and charged. A youth probation officer requested that the sentencing judge include meetings with the victims as part of the sentence. A meeting was organized by the Mennonite Central Committee and the probation officer. Following the meeting, the youths agreed to pay for the damages. And perhaps more importantly, they also came face to face with the consequences of their actions:

> Meeting our victims was one of the hardest things I had ever done in my entire life. Accompanied by Mark Yantzi (our probation officer) and Dave Worth (a volunteer), we walked up to the victims front door to apologize, hear what the victims had to say, determine the amount of restitution, ask for forgiveness and assure the victims that they were not targeted. It was a random act of vandalism.
>
> Some victims offered forgiveness while others wanted to give us a good whipping. Nonetheless, we survived meeting the victims of our crime spree and returned a couple of months later with certified cheques to restore the amount of out-of-pocket expenses not covered by insurance. The total damage was around $2,200; my accomplice and myself each had to pay $550 restitution and each paid a $200 fine. (Kelly n.d.)

This incident led to the development of the Kitchener Victim-Offender Reconciliation Program, still in operation today and credited as the origin of the restorative justice movement in Canada (Peachey 1989).

An organized meeting between the victims and offenders as part of a court sentence was groundbreaking. The meeting provided an opportunity for the victims to participate in the reparations and for the offenders to hear first-hand how their actions had affected others. Russell Kelly, one of the youths involved in that first victim-offenders meeting, has since graduated from college and joined Community Justice Initiatives, a restorative justice program in Kitchener. According to Kelly, working in restorative justice was "meant to be" (Kelly n.d.).

In the mid-1980s, the small Ojibway town of Hollow Water, Manitoba, similarly began to experiment with restorative justice. The community was experiencing the effects of alcoholism, violence, and incest. Joyce Bushie, who lived in Hollow Water, describes the problems faced by her community prior to the development of the healing circles (Bushie 1997). Alcohol and violence, both physical and sexual, were destroying people's lives. She describes the point at which some of them stopped drinking and started to discuss the origins of their problems. As time passed more people became involved, and the community started to confront the real abuse happening all around them. They came to recognize the cycle of abuse that led people abused as children to become abusers themselves. Bushie (1997) describes how sharing the burden of the abuse was the first step in healing.

Healing circles have been held in Hollow Water ever since. The community is recognized internationally as a successful model of a restorative justice approach to crime and community conflict.

## Restorative Justice

Restorative justice defines crime as a violation of social or interpersonal relationships, rather than a violation of an official rule or regulation. Crime, or "wrongdoing," undermines social relationships, potentially harming individuals, groups, and communities (Walgrave 2005, 5). Restorative justice addresses the harm that results from a crime; in this wholesale shift in thinking about wrongdoing, the common belief that justice is best achieved through punishment and retribution is challenged.

Howard Zehr, an early proponent of the modern restorative justice movement, outlines three underlying assumptions:

1 .crime violates relationships
2. these violations create obligations and liabilities

3. justice should heal and "make right" the relationships that have been harmed by the crime.

Source: Zehr 2002, 19

According to Zehr, restorative justice is not so much a program or a policy as it is a "set of guiding beliefs" that underpins an innovative response to crime (Woolford 2009, 41). Victims, offenders, and members of the community are brought together to address wrongdoing (Zehr 2002, 25).

The United Nations definition similarly emphasizes the involvement of victims, offenders, and community members. Here, restorative justice consists of

> any process in which the victim and the offender, and where appropriate, any other individuals or community members affected by a crime, participate together actively in the resolution of matters arising from the crime, generally with the help of a facilitator. (United Nations Economic and Social Council 2000, 40–41)

Similarly, for Tony Marshall, restorative justice is "a process whereby all the parties with a stake in a particular offence come together to resolve collectively how to deal with the aftermath of the offence and its implications for the future" (Marshall 1999, 5).

## The View from a Restorative Justice Advocate

Kay Pranis is a leader in the restorative justice movement in North America. She has trained people around the world in using restorative justice in settings ranging from schools to prisons. About the involvement of community, she states:

> Over the past twenty years of work in restorative justice, the importance of community involvement has become increasingly clear. . . . RJ [restorative justice] recognizes that communities, not just individuals, are victimized and consequently there is a need for healing and repair of communities. RJ also recognizes that communities bear responsibility for some of the conditions that foster crime resulting in an obligation on the part of the community to address underlying causes of crime. And finally, RJ recognizes that communities have more influence on behaviour than the criminal justice system and therefore are an essential force in responding to and reducing criminal behaviour. (Pranis 2010)

# The View from a Victim

Restorative justice can be a powerful experience. Even victims of serious crimes may eventually come to forgive offenders. Katy Hutchinson's husband was killed when he went to a neighbour's house to investigate an unruly party. She has written about her subsequent experiences with the young man who was convicted of the crime.

> I've been able to forgive Ryan because of the immense sympathy I have for his mother. I understood her loss. We haven't met yet but we write and I cherish her letters. Forgiveness isn't easy. . . . Whether victim or perpetrator, part of being human is rolling up our sleeves and taking an active part in repairing harm.
>
> Emma and Sam [my two children] have fully supported my choice to forgive Ryan, but others have asked, "How could you?" Bob's friends especially took a long time to understand how I could move on with my life. But something happened when Bob died and I found my voice. Forgiveness became an opportunity to create a new and hopeful beginning.

Source: Hutchinson 2010

According to these definitions, victim participation is integral to the work of restorative justice; describing the experience of a particular event is the backbone of the process. In a traditional court process, victims are witnesses to the crime who help the prosecution make the case against the accused. In some cases, victims have the opportunity to read victim impact statements, but by and large they are not involved in decisions about the case or its outcome.

The involvement of victims may help offenders to understand the consequences of their actions. Offenders are held to a higher standard of accountability than if they had pleaded guilty in court. In a traditional court setting, the offender passively receives the judge's decision. In a restorative justice process, the offender comes face-to-face with the effect of their actions on the victim or victims.

Restorative justice processes define victims broadly. Members of the community in which a crime has taken place may participate, even though they were not the primary victims. They may still experience negative effects or feel harmed by a particular incident. Restorative justice programs are also typically run by community-based agencies. In this way, it is the community, rather than criminal justice agencies, that is responding to crime.

Restorative justice is achieved through various processes—sometimes called "encounters" or conferences—that bring together people affected by the crime. Facilitators help with the meetings, allowing participants to "explore facts, feelings, and resolutions" (Zehr 2002, 45). Facilitators may be professionals or trained volunteers. In some cases it may not be appropriate for the victim and offender to meet; a facilitator can instead help coordinate other forms of communication, such as letters. However the communication takes place, the goal is to allow those affected by the offence to share their perspective. The process will ideally produce some agreement on reparation, hold the offender accountable, and provide a sense of closure. The victim may even come to forgive the offender.

## The Practice of Restorative Justice

Restorative justice practices all have in common certain key characteristics. A wide range of people, including victims, offenders, and community members, work together collaboratively (Zehr 2002, 25). Facilitators help participants express their concerns and tell their stories, but they do not act as mediators or arbitrators. Participation in restorative justice must be voluntary. In particular, the offender needs to take responsibility for his or her actions and agree to participate in restorative justice. In all its forms, restorative justice processes aim to produce an outcome which, as much as possible, all participants can accept (Zehr 2002, 25). Processes differ depending on who is included in the encounter and the depth of intervention involved.

Victim-offender conferences bring victims and offenders together with facilitators who guide them through conversations about reparation. Victims describe their experiences, and offenders become aware of the consequences of their behaviour (Cooley 2002, 4). Reparations might include apologies or financial restitution; offenders may be asked to do work for the victim or for a charity or community group.

Family group conferences involve more participants, including members of the victims' or offenders' families or other supporters. The conferences may also include relevant officials such as police and social workers. The participants recall the event and its effects, and reparation is discussed (Cooley 2002, 5). This model is particularly focused on "supporting offenders in taking responsibility and changing their behaviour" (Zehr 2002, 48). The community can show disapproval of the offender, but at the same time they help support the offender's efforts at reparation and reintegration into the community (Cooley 2002, 5). In some cases, family group conferences go beyond reparation. In New Zealand, for example, family group conferences are used as part of a larger plan to address underlying issues (Zehr 2002, 50).

Peacemaking, or healing, circles are another forum (Stuart 1997). Drawing from traditional practices and principles of conflict resolution in Aboriginal communities, these circles constitute an ongoing process of healing rather than a single meeting or conversation (Stuart and Pranis 2008). Participants must be properly prepared for the circle and debriefed afterward. Participants take turns talking in the order of seating, without interrupting other speakers. Those who do not wish to speak can pass. The goal is to facilitate communication allowing participants to develop a shared understanding and agree on how best to move forward.

## Restorative Justice in Canada

Restorative justice is built into Canadian legislation and jurisprudence. The Principles of Sentencing, described in Chapter 2, include two relevant sections. Section 718(e) provides for "reparations done to victims or the community" and Section 718(f) states that sentencing should promote "a sense of responsibility in offenders, and acknowledgment of the harm done to victims and the community." The Youth Criminal Justice Act also includes provisions for restorative justice at the time of charging or sentencing. The Supreme Court of Canada has referred to "restorative" forms of sentencing in two important cases interpreting these two sections of the Criminal Code.[2] These cases provided some definitions of restorative justice and endorsed it as a reasonable response to crime. Such formal recognition of restorative approaches provide the opportunity for all sectors of the justice system—police, courts, and corrections—to play a role in developing a more effective response to crime.

Police forces in Canada have been widely involved with restorative justice programs. The RCMP, for example, has developed Community Justice Forums, a process that closely resembles family group conferences and peacemaking circles (Richards 2000). Police officers participate in restorative justice sessions in areas that have restorative justice programs. In Nova Scotia—home to one of the most comprehensive restorative justice programs in North America—police officers make referrals to community-based restorative justice agencies in cases where restorative justice is deemed appropriate. The Halifax Regional Police also has a Youth Court Officer who ensures that officers are making appropriate referrals (in other words, not sending cases to court when restorative justice would be more appropriate). Many police agencies are thus seeing the merits of a non-punitive response to crime and integrating restorative justice into their work.

Some judges play a key role in promoting restorative justice in Canada. Beginning in the early 1990s in the Yukon, Judge Barry Stuart instituted sentencing circles to solicit community input on the sentences

# The View from a Police Chief

Vern White, chief of police in Ottawa, promotes restorative justice as a response to crime and a means of resolving problems within the police organization himself. He states that:

In 29 years of policing I have been exposed to many aspects of justice that work and many more that fail. In this period of time there is one area more than any other where I have seen real justice and success. That area is r estorative justice. It has been successful in a number of areas and they include:

1. Victim satisfaction: I have witnessed the positive impact restorative justice has made on victims and the sense of ownership and value they gain from a truly victim focused justice system.
2. Recidivism: Many researchers have argued that recidivism rates are impacted by who is selected to participate, but in my research and that conducted by others, we have seen reduced recidivism rates, sometimes by as much as half.
3. Community involvement: The impact of the community and their sense of ownership of restorative justice cannot be overemphasized. I have seen the impact that the community can have on both the offender and the victim in resolving conflict and restoring a sense of calm to all those involved in the offence.

Source: White 2010

for Aboriginal offenders. Today, Canadian judges may use sentencing circles at their discretion; they are most widely used in cases involving Aboriginal offenders. The hope is that sentencing circles will help reduce the disproportionate incarceration of Aboriginal offenders and provide a more culturally sensitive response. Judges can use their discretion to include restorative justice in their decisions, but the programs available vary widely across the provinces. For example, Nova Scotia is the only province in which judges can divert young offenders out of court to a community-based restorative justice agency.

Sentencing circles are perhaps the most widely publicized—and criticized—form of restorative justice. They have attracted some negative reactions, particularly in cases involving serious crimes. The case of Christopher Pauchay brought the issue to the fore. He was charged in the death of his two daughters who died of hypothermia after being left outside in only diapers and t-shirts on a winter night (Pauchey had been drinking heavily). A sentencing circle of 23 people, including the two girls' mother, recommended that Pauchay receive treatment for drug and alcohol addiction and participate in spiritual activities. The judge rejected the recommendation, arguing that the sentence was not proportionate to the crime; instead, he sentenced Pauchay to a three-year prison term (Adam 2009). This case reveals the tensions between a decision made by the community and the ultimate authority of a judge working in a retributive system.

Correctional Service of Canada is heavily involved with the development and promotion of restorative justice. An annual "Restorative Justice Week" is run by CSC. The agency also produces a compilation of restorative justice programs across the country and evaluates restorative justice projects, with the goal of designing correctional programs that incorporate some key principles.[3]

In addition to research, CSC has designed a project that assesses the applicability of restorative justice processes and practices in a prison setting. In 2001 restorative units were set up in the Grande Cache prison in Alberta, involving victim-offender mediation (Petrellis 2007). Currently, CSC offers the Restorative Opportunities program. Victims, offenders, or community members may participate in various forms of communication, using restorative justice models.

Community groups run many restorative justice programs across Canada. In Nova Scotia, community-based agencies take referrals from all levels of the justice system—police, Crown, court, and corrections.[4] The agencies are run by community boards to administer the provincial restorative justice program. The program itself is run as a partnership between the Department of Justice and community agencies. In Alberta, citizen groups can establish Justice Committees, which are sanctioned by local judges and Crowns but usually run by volunteers; there are over 120 active Justice Committees. Across the country, many chapters of the John Howard Society run restorative justice programs. The Church Council on Justice and Corrections and the Mennonite Central Committee are also involved with restorative justice in a range of contexts. In cities across Canada, small community-based non-profit agencies run restorative justice programs either as alternatives to traditional criminal justice or as programs that operate alongside the existing system.

Another innovative restorative justice program involves high-risk sex offenders. Circles of Support and Accountability (COSA) provide support to offenders who are leaving prison at the end of their sentence and are at a high risk to reoffend. These offenders have not served any time on parole, and their release creates considerable anxiety in the community. COSAs originated in faith-based organizations whose members wanted to decrease the social isolation and exclusion experienced by

## The View from an Inmate

Todd Blomquist served a 27-month sentence for trafficking. He describes his experiences in the restorative justice unit of the Grande Cache prison:

> Living on the [Restorative Justice] Unit has given me the perfect environment to start my rehabilitation and preparation for reintegration to a better life. . . .
>
> I had the pleasure of being involved in a very special three-day peacemaking circle which had some very eye-opening activities. I had the chance to open up to the group and share some memories and emotions that had been barriers to my progress. . . .
>
> Because of the peacemaking circles I attended and still attend, I have come to realize the impact of my crimes. As many of my victims are addicts, I have had the unique opportunity to see the impact that drugs has [sic] had on other offenders and their families. Through seeing this, I learned to acknowledge the ripple effect I created with my crimes, the primary victims and secondary victims involved. . . .
>
> I owe a lot of my success to the [restorative justice] philosophy, the circles and the peer support I receive on the Unit. I know the real test will be when I leave here, but I know I now have the tools to succeed and it's thanks to restorative justice.

Source: Blomquist 2004

many high-risk offenders upon release from prison. They believed that this isolation and exclusion set the stage for the ex-inmates to reoffend.

The first Circle began in 1994. Led by Harry Nigh, a Mennonite pastor, the Circle was set up to provide support for a sex offender named Charlie Taylor. Taylor was being released after serving a seven-year sentence for several offences against children. It was his fourth time in jail for similar offences. Harry Nigh set up a group of concerned community members to help reintegrate Taylor into the community and provide him with the support needed to prevent him from reoffending. Taylor remained connected to the Circle until his death in 2006. He never did reoffend. There are now a hundred Circles being run by 20 organizations across the country. Correctional Service of Canada oversees the programs by developing training programs for COSA participants and undertaking research on their outcomes (The Church Council on Justice and Corrections 2008).

In COSAs, members of the community come together with offenders to help them stay accountable and to find safe ways to reintegrate. COSAs involve four to seven well-trained volunteers who work with high-risk offenders as they reintegrate into the community. Circle

# The View from the Church Council on Justice and Corrections

Rita Scott is a Crown Attorney who sits on the board of the Church Council on Justice and Corrections. She provided testimony about restorative justice to the Parliamentary Standing Committee on Justice and Human Rights. She describes a particularly provocative case:

I want to tell you specifically about one incident that happened when a young girl in the high school phoned in bomb threats to the school. It was a joke. She was hanging out with a bunch of her friends. They were taking the afternoon off school. They thought this would be funny. What they didn't realize is that the principal of the secondary school where this happened had a four-month-old child in the day care centre in that school. He was, needless to say, freaked by what was going on, torn between "What do I do about the safety of my child, when I want to pick up my baby and run out of here with that kid" and "How do I discharge my obligations for the safety of everybody in the school?"

The matter went on and was investigated. The accused kid was identified. A process unfolded. The high school principal was very keen that we should use this process of family group conferencing. We brought together the kid, her family, the others who had been with her that day, the secretary who answered the phone, some of the teachers who had been present at the time and evacuated the school, the police officer who dealt with it, and the principal. We all sat around in a circle. We talked about it in an organized and sensitive way and in a very honest way.

When that young woman saw the high school principal in tears talking about this terrible dilemma that he had been in and what that process was like, it was the biggest shock in the world to her. But it was a process that would never have happened in the court system. She would never have had to say a word. Nobody would have understood what was going on. She would probably have never known what that had been like for the person she really most seriously affected.

There was a terrific outcome from it. I could go on about the work she did in the day care centre, the stuff she did to convince others that those kinds of foolish, mindless things that you do on the spur of the moment can have long-lasting effects, etc., but obviously that was a defining moment for that young woman, and also for the high school principal, who got a better sense of how things like that could occur than he ever had before. They had an incredible opportunity for resolution and healing that never would have happened in the court system.

Source: Scott 2000

members meet regularly over a long period of time to support offenders and help prevent them from reoffending. Wilson, Picheca, and Prinzo (2005, 2) note that, "A COSA is a relationship scheme based on friendship and accountability. . . . COSAs have become surrogate families for many core members [i.e., the offenders]." Thus, insofar as they maintain offender accountability and emphasize reintegration and

## The View from a Circle

Wray Budreo, called "one of Canada's most notorious pedophiles" by the *Toronto Star* (Dunphy 2007), had been in and out of prison for 30 years. In 1993 he was released; highly publicized protests against his release were staged by the community in which he planned to live. Members of the Toronto Mennonite Central Committee set up a COSA that lasted until Budreo's death in 2007.

One member of the COSA was Detective Wendy Leaver of the Metropolitan Toronto Police sexual assault squad. When asked to join the COSA she reflects that, "My initial response to myself was, 'I put these people in jail. I don't support them when they come out of the system. . . . Do these individual (forming circles) have any idea what they're dealing with, or are they just a bunch of tree huggers?'" (Dunphy 2007). Detective Leaver joined the circle primarily to have some control over Budreo. Since then she has come to value the benefits of the circle, and has joined two others.

community engagement, the Circles incorporate many of the ideas of restorative justice.

In terms of wider social justice, the Truth and Reconciliation Commission of Canada for residential schools students represents a large-scale restorative justice effort at the national level. Residential schools were established in the 1920s to help the Catholic and Protestant churches achieve their goal of "civilizing" the Aboriginal population (Monture-Angus 1999). Conditions in the schools were abysmal. A generation of Aboriginal children experienced verbal, physical, and sexual abuse. In many Aboriginal communities today, the devastation of this abuse has led to an ongoing cycle of violence and abuse. High rates of addiction and suicide are other markers of what Woolford calls "intergenerational trauma" (2009, 56). Members of the Truth and Reconciliation Commission travel across Canada to hear the stories of those affected by the residential school system. The record of their findings will be public. The Honourable Justice Murray Sinclair, Chair of the Truth and Reconcilliation Commission, describes the work of the Commisssion:

> We, at the Commission, are aware of the degree to which the inter-generational survivors, the current children and grandchildren of survivors, hunger for more than just knowing why. We know that they also hunger for a proper sense of self. The need to assist current and future generations of Indigenous youth to find their place and purpose through cultural and language revitalization is quite apparent. Indigenous children are much more than the colour of

their skin, they are the products of their community and they have the right to know what that community is. (Sinclair 2010)

## Evaluating Restorative Justice

The principles and practices of restorative justice are closely aligned with three of the utilitarian goals outlined in Chapter 2: providing reparations for harm, promoting a sense of responsibility in offenders, and assisting with rehabilitation. Restorative justice processes are designed to find ways for offenders to make amends and to take responsibility for their actions. These goals, which are not part of traditional criminal justice responses to crime, are built into both the principles and the practices of restorative justice.

Restorative justice does not try to rehabilitate offenders, but research suggests that it can complement treatment and rehabilitative programs. One thorough study of the available literature concluded that restorative justice enhances the satisfaction of victims and offenders. Used in conjunction with treatment, the study found that restorative justice "enable[s] both approaches [treatment and restorative justice] to capitalize on their strengths and minimize their weaknesses" (Latimer, Dowden, and Muise 2005, 18). Another study found that restorative justice programs have better psychological outcomes than traditional criminal justice responses (Poulson 2003). Restorative justice complements treatment by opening the door to personal transformation and opportunities for healing (Zehr 2002, 17).

Research suggests that many restorative justice programs do successfully reduce recidivism (Latimer, Dowden, and Muise 2005). The most effective programs in this regard are highly structured and appear to work best with low-risk offenders (Bonta et al. 2008). Correctional Service of Canada has evaluated the effectiveness of COSAs in reducing expected recidivism rates for high-risk offenders; the conclusion is that participation in a COSA reduces reoffending rates (Wilson, Picheca, and Prinzo 2005; 2007).

Restorative justice appears to be cost effective—it costs less than other traditional responses (Sherman and Strang 2007). Other savings come from diverting offenders from court and prisons. It may also reduce the health-care costs related to the trauma and psychological effects of crime (Sherman and Strang 2007, 86).

Despite these positive findings, critics of restorative justice suggest it is "soft" on crime—that it fails to be properly retributive. Indeed, some restorative justice advocates see it as a "paradigm shift" away from retributive justice (Zehr 1990). The retributive criminal justice system, they argue, is too adversarial. It ignores the needs of victims and allows offenders to take a passive role. Zehr (1990) is also critical of the traditional criminal justice focus on blame and guilt, imposing punishment and pain as a deterrent against future offending. What critics find to be a weakness, advocates see as a key strength.

Others suggest that the distinction between restorative justice and retributive justice has been exaggerated (Daly 2000). These commentators point out that we can think about retribution as being more about hardship than punishment (Llewellyn and Howse 1998, 38). Restorative justice can be difficult, requiring a great deal of those who participate; it is often demanding, if not punishing (Walgrave 2004). Llewellyn and Howse (1999) make another connection between the two, arguing that restorative justice, like retributive justice, aims to achieve an equitable outcome. Retributive justice achieves equitable consequences based on historical practices of punishment. Restorative justice, on the other hand, brings people together to discuss the most appropriate response to the particular incident.

Restoriatve justice offers a new vision for the practice of justice in liberal democracies. Rather than justice being what the state does to us, it can be something that we do together. Those who have participated in restorative justice tend to perceive it as fair (Daly 2000). Restorative justice programs are highly accountable to the public given the key role of community participation. This participation also allows for more transparency. For these reasons, restorative justice has the potential to create a fairer, more equitable, more effective justice system.

By offering communities more input, restorative justice may improve public confidence. In Chapter 1 we saw a public lack of confidence in the Canadian criminal justice system. We also saw that the public prioritizes accountability and reparation over deterrence and denunciation. The goals of restorative justice more closely match the goals that Canadians believe should be achieved by the justice system. Restorative justice may offer some solutions to some of the most intractable problems in our system: inequity, cost, recidivism, and the apparent contradiction between our social values and our punitive response to crime.

# Where Do We Go from Here?

## Current Government Priorities

In the past few years crime control has been a major focus for the Canadian government. Since 2006, when the Conservatives won their first minority, the government has repeatedly tried to pass several major pieces of legislation related to crime. Some passed, while others were held up by the majority opposition. Many of the bills focused on increasing the penalties for certain crimes and restricting the rights of offenders, particularly those in prisons. The government succeeded in passing bills to extend the period of parole eligibility for multiple murders (Bill C-48),[1] eliminating the faint hope clause[2] for those convicted of murder, and ending the practice of two-for-one credit for time served. Certainly, crime and measures to control it have been widely debated in Parliament and in the media in recent years.

We have seen other changes since the Conservatives came into power. Spending in Correctional Service of Canada has increased considerably, by over 90 percent since 2006.[3] Despite cutbacks in other areas, spending and staffing at CSC continues to increase (Correctional Service of Canada 2010a; 2011). The government has established the Federal Ombudsman for Victims of Crime, developed the National Anti-Drug Strategy,[4] and funded an increase in the number of police officers across the country.

During the 2011 election campaign, the Conservative Party made several commitments related to crime. They promised to propose an omnibus crime bill within one hundred days of winning an election.

This bill will merge 12 bills from the earlier session of Parliament, including restrictions on the use of house arrest with conditional sentences (previously Bill C-16), a reduction in the availability of pardons (previously Bill C-23B), restrictions on parole eligibility (previously Bill C-39), and two bills leading to mandatory minimum sentences (previously Bill C-54 and S-10).[5] They also promised to eliminate the long-gun registry. In their election platform, *Here for Canada*,[6] the Conservative Party laid out four priority areas:

1. Supporting victims of crime;
2. Eliminating drugs in prison;
3. Combating human trafficking;
4. Ending sentence discounts for multiple child pornography and sex offences.

These promises, and the past activities of the Conservative government, have tended to revolve around several key priorities. Victims have been placed front and centre on the government's crime control agenda. One major goal has been to increase punishments and change sentencing practices (the bills proposing mandatory sentences are just one example). These changes are part of a broader goal to increase offender accountability. Prisons have also been a key focus. The government is investing heavily in an expansion of the federal prison system. Proposed changes to parole eligibility and promises to implement mandatory drug testing for inmates are targeting the perceived lack of offender accountability. The issue of drugs in prison relates to another key aspect of the government's crime control agenda—increased punishments for some drug offences and a shift away from harm-reduction policies both in prisons and in the community.

The government suggests that we should be concerned about crime despite falling crime rates. In a 2008 speech Stephen Harper stated that "we are working hard to make our country and our communities safer. Canadians feel less safe than they once did. They rightly worry about the security of their neighbourhoods and their nation." He went on to suggest that Canadians' experiences contradict the numbers:

Some try to pacify Canadians with statistics. "Your personal experiences and impressions are wrong," they say; "crime is really not a problem." These apologists remind me of the scene in the Wizard of Oz when the wizard says, "Pay no attention to that man behind the curtain." But Canadians can see behind the curtain. They know there's a problem. (cited in Wherry 2010)

Similarly, in a web posting in July 2010, then Minister of Public Safety Vic Toews reasserted an argument made by Sun Media columnist Lorrie Goldstein. Goldstein questions the assertion that crime has gone down, pointing out that violent crime rates have tripled since 1962[7] (Toews 2010). Unreported crime has also been raised as a concern. When he was President of Treasury Board in 2010, Stockwell Day was asked to explain why the government will increase spending on prisons when crime rates are falling: "[p]eople simply aren't reporting the same way they used to. . . . One statistic of many that concerns us is the amount of crimes that go unreported. Those numbers are alarming and it shows that we can't take a liberal view to crime" (cited in CTV Ottawa 2010). Two other prominent cabinet ministers, Vic Toews (2010) and Rob Nicholson (cited in CTV 2010), supported Day's observations. Toews (2010) concluded that because "[i]ncreasingly larger numbers of Canadians are no longer reporting crimes to the police meaning statistics showing that the crime rate is falling are fundamentally flawed." The government continues to promote the view that the official crime rate is hiding the reality of crime in Canada.

The government also justifies crime policies by invoking the needs and desires of victims. In September 2010, then Public Safety Minister Vic Toews stated clearly that victims support their policies:

Mr. Speaker, in fact, we are listening to victims. And victims want dangerous, repeat criminals in prison. They want safe streets. They don't want the dangerous criminals on the streets. And they want laws that target the criminals. They don't believe that the long-gun registry targets criminals. In fact, it targets law-abiding hunters and farmers and sportspeople right across this country. It's not a law we need in Canada. (Wherry 2010)

Toews again emphasized the need to support victims when he announced the expansion of prisons in British Columbia:

Our Government is proud to be on the right side of this issue— the side of law-abiding citizens, the side of victims who want justice, and the side that understands the cost of a safe and secure society is an investment worth making. (Correctional Service of Canada 2010c)

Stephen Harper has also evoked the concerns of victims when asked to defend the costs of the government's crime control agenda: "Taking the bad guys out of circulation for a while, does it cost money? . . .Yes. Is it worth it? Yes, just ask the victim" (cited in McKie 2011). Such a statement implies that offenders' rights have somehow been prioritized over those of victims.

Claiming concern over excessive rights for offenders is part of the government's law and order agenda. Offender accountability was a major theme in the CSC Review Panel Report (2007, see Chapter 3). A key aspect here is changes in the parole system, restricting access to what they call "early" parole. Then Minister of Justice Vic Toews claimed:

> Our Government agrees with Canadians—the corrections and conditional release system should put public safety first. . . . The punishment should fit the crime, and the rights of criminals should not come ahead of the rights of victims and law-abiding citizens. (cited in Public Safety Canada 2010)

Here again we see the themes common to other arguments in support of Conservative government policies: safety, punishment, and foregrounding victims' rights over those of offenders.

## Research and Government Policies

Contrary to statements from ministers quoted earlier, surveys have shown that Canadians are in fact feeling increasingly safe (Gannon 2004; Perrault and Brennan 2010; Roberts 2001). The 2009 General Social Survey found that 93 percent of those polled said that they were somewhat or very satisfied with their level of personal safety (Perrault and Brennan 2010). This represents an increase since the 1994 GSS, which found that 86 percent of respondents were somewhat or very satisfied (Gannon 2004). Ninety percent of Canadians reported feeling safe walking alone in their neighbourhood at night; this number has remained unchanged since 2004 (Perrault and Brennan 2010).While foregrounding the false perception that the public feels unsafe, the government continues to ignore the very real problem of public confidence in the system (see discussion in Chapter 1).

Another false assumption relates to unreported crime. Chapter 1 describes how data on unreported crime comes from victimization surveys, gathered by the GSS. According to the GSS, the victimization rate in Canada has changed very little since 1993. Consistently we see that about one-quarter of Canadians report having been victimized at some point in the 12 months prior to the survey. We are not seeing an explosion of unreported crimes.

Rates of reporting to police have decreased slightly over time. In 1993, 42 percent of crimes reported in the GSS had been reported to the police (Besserer and Trainor 2000). By 2009 that had decreased to 31 percent (Perrault and Brennan 2010). Violent victimization was more likely to be reported than property crimes. Sexual assault was the least likely crime to have been reported—88 percent of sexual assaults reported in the survey had not been brought to the attention of the police. Among other crimes, theft of personal property and household property theft were the least likely crimes to have been reported (Perrault and Brennan 2010).

Each year the survey asks respondents why they did not report the crime. The most typical answer is that the incident was not serious enough to involve the police. The decrease in reporting may be worth addressing in policy, or we may accept that the incidents really are too minor to require the attention of the criminal justice system. Either way, the Conservative government's crime control agenda does not address the problem of underreporting. They have not targeted the least reported offences in any of their policies or planned policies; there is no reference to crimes such as sexual assault that disproportionately affect women.

As seen in the earlier discussion, concern over crime rates is also used to support the tough-on-crime policies advocated by the current government. As we saw in Chapter 1, the official crime rate, compiled from police statistics, peaked in 1991 and has generally been decreasing since then. Our crime rate is now as low as it was in the mid-1970s and has been decreasing over the past two decades.

Another important point is that few of the current policies and proposed policies are supported by research; some of their proponents in fact seem to be turning their backs outright on research. Earlier chapters saw proposed changes to parole are not supported by what we have learned about the importance of gradual release. Harm-reduction initiatives have also been rejected by the government, in spite of their successes, as documented by the federal agencies tasked to research such questions. Earlier chapters have also shown that some approaches to crime control better reflect our social values. Chapter 3 explored how increased use of prison is unlikely to be cost efficient, and that research shows that deterrence-based sentencing has no positive outcome. Chapter 7 explored restorative justice, a far cry from the retributive polices in favour with our government, although it reduces reoffending and increases victim satisfaction.

Other research speaks directly to the policies, legislative changes, and proposals described above. Mandatory minimum sentences are a particular problem in this regard. The US experience has shown that mandatory sentences have had unintended consequences, and research has found that they fail to achieve their goals (Gendreau, Goggin, and Cullen 1999; Tonry 2009). One large study that drew on over 50 other studies concluded that increased imprisonment, which results from mandatory minimum sentences, does not reduce recidivism (Gendreau, Goggin, and Cullen 1999). This study is described on the Public Safety Canada website; however, there remains a large discrepancy between the research described by Public Safety and CSC, and press releases announcing government initiatives.

The positioning of mandatory minimum sentences on government web pages suggests that the Conservative government is not pursuing research-based policies. Another example furthers this point. In 2009 a reporter for *Maclean's* invited then Justice Minister Rob Nicholson to provide data in support of proposed mandatory sentences (Geddes 2009). In an article about crime policies, the reporter quotes a memo received in response from the minister's office: "The studies are inconclusive particularly with respect to the main debate: do MMPs [mandatory minimum penalties] deter crime?" (Geddes 2009).

Cost is another problem associated with the current crime control agenda. The Parliamentary Budget Officer has estimated that Bill C-25, the Truth in Sentencing Act, will cost between seven and ten billion dollars, more than twice the estimates provided by the government (Rajekar and Mathilakath 2010). Restrictions on parole and conditional sentencing will also cost money by requiring more offenders to be housed inside prisons for longer rather than in the community. Provinces are also worried about the costs given that many of the crime bills will increase the number of inmates held in provincial institutions (Galloway 2011). The government has not provided cost estimates for these initiatives and questions remain about their efficacy.

Earlier we saw that Stephen Harper justified the costs by suggesting that his government's policies meet the needs and expectations of victims of crime. While many victims' rights group do call for harsh penalties, others take a more nuanced approach. The Canadian Resource Centre for Victims of Crime, for example, does not support the current government agenda.[8] Furthermore, both the past and current Ombudsmen for Victims of Crime have raised concerns. The current ombudsman has suggested that not all victims support the elimination of the long-gun registry (cited in Wherry 2010). The past ombudsman is outspoken in his criticism of the current government's approach:

> [J]ustice is about more than how much we punish offenders. That narrow view ignores the majority of victims of violent crime, victims of sexual assault and child victims who never report their crimes. There is lots the opposition parties could be doing to demand action from the government on important justice related

issues. They could put forward a series of justice initiatives (I have some ideas), that focus on victims and crime prevention and high risk offenders, that the current government is not doing because it is spending billions on getting tougher on crime. Give Canadians an alternative vision of justice. To do so will take the courage to challenge the public perceptions of crime and a real commitment because real solutions are not explained in simple soundbites, nor will they be solved with a bill or a press conference—they take time. (Sullivan 2010)

Others have questioned the government's real commitment to victims. Justin Piché has pointed out that while the government boasts increased funding to victims' issues, it has cut funding to victim-related programs such as the Grants for Victims of Crime Initiative among others.

To be sure, other organizations in Canada have opposed Conservative government policies. Many community-based organizations support alternatives to traditional forms of criminal justice responses. Others, such as victims' groups, oppose the current government focus on retribution and punishment. Another organization, the Church Council on Justice and Corrections, for example, has complained that increasing the number of people being sent to prisons is costly and ineffective:

The Canadian government has regretfully embraced a belief in punishment-for-crime that first requires us to isolate and separate the offender from the rest of us, in our minds as well as in our prisons. That separation makes what happens later easier to ignore. . . . Increasing levels of incarceration of marginalized people is counter-productive and undermines human dignity in our society. By contrast, well-supervised probation or release, bail options, reporting centres, practical assistance, supportive housing, programs that promote accountability, respect and reparation: these measures have all been well-established but they are underfunded. (cited in Piché 2010)

A final problem with the current agenda is that it diverts attention away from several pressing issues. Chapter 3 explored our continued failure to deal with the disproportionate number of incarcerated Aboriginal peoples. Mental health and lack of programming in Canadian prisons is another problem. The growing number of people held in remand is reaching crisis proportions; the federal government has not proposed any measures to address this. In fact, many of their policies will exacerbate the problem of large numbers in inmates held in provincial custody serving sentences of less than two years. Addressing these issues will require cooperation from the provinces and perhaps changes to the administration of custodial institutions in Canada.

The current government's crime control agenda is based on a false assumption about Canadian's fear of crime and the level of unreported crime, coupled with untrue claims that decreasing police-reported crime rates hide that reality of crime. The agenda ignores both research and the views of community-based agencies (including victims' rights groups), and will be very expensive. Why then is the government intent on implementing their crime control agenda?

## The Politics of Crime Control

Pursuing tough-on-crime policies is politically expedient. The Conservative Party's policies have been the focus of this book, but the other main political parties in Canada also use similar rhetoric. No political party wants to appear "soft" on crime.

Ian Brodie, Stephen Harper's former chief of staff, candidly described the politicization of crime policies in Canada:

> Every time we proposed amendments to the Criminal Code, sociologists, criminologists, defence lawyers and Liberals attacked us for proposing measures that the evidence apparently showed did not work. . . . That was a good thing for us politically, in that sociologists, criminologists and defence lawyers were and are all held in lower repute than Conservative politicians by the voting public. Politically it helped us tremendously to be attacked by this coalition of university types. (quote in Geddes 2009)

Crime control policies have been politicized so much that research has become irrelevant. But Canadians would be outraged if politicians dismissed research when approving the safety and effectiveness of new drugs.

To be sure, many Canadians agree with specific policies. Polls have found that a large proportion of Canadians agree with mandatory sentences for drug offences, for example (Angus Reid 2009b). But recall also that Chapter 4 explored how Canadians may lack sufficient information to make a decision about conditional sentences. Chapter 1 also showed the discrepancy between what people perceive as the typical sentence and how they themselves would sentence a particular offender. Consider too that the public is generally ill-informed about actual sentencing patterns—we hear only of extreme cases in the media. It may be that there is something inherently appealing about an apparently simple solution, such as mandatory sentences.

Would Canadians support these polices if they knew the full context? Chapter 1 saw how Canadians prioritized accountability and reparation over punishment and deterrence. They also support alternatives to prison. How then is it that such policies continue to be politically expedient?

Consider comments made by Frank Graves following the last election about why his public opinion polls did not adequately predict the Conservative government majority. Polls, he argued, do not accurately represent the view of those Canadians who choose to vote. In other words, in his view, the election results do not properly represent the values and views of most Canadians (Valpy 2011). The same might be true for polls that measure the values of Canadians as they relate to the criminal justice system. Our values may not be well reflected in our politics because of the demographic who votes. Crime policies may have been a classic wedge issue.

## Where Do We Go from Here?

There are some key successes in our criminal justice policies. For all its failings, our system is still a model for the world. Our parole system works well. Chapter 4 described how breach rates have been decreasing over time, but Canadians still have very little confidence in the system. Perhaps more education is needed on the success of our programs. Chapter 3 saw that Canada has developed treatment models that are world renowned. Improved funding for and access to these programs would ultimately serve public safety well. Chapter 7 saw that our restorative justice programs are widely recognized to be innovative and effective.

It is also important to recognize that beginning with the Canadian Sentencing Commission in 1987 our criminal justice system has tended to move away from mandatory sentences, discouraged the use of prison for most offenders, and promoted the use of gradual release from prisons. If we believe that policies can reduce crime, then we might conclude that we have been moving in the right direction, and we might stay the course rather than shifting to a more punitive and retributive system.

# Notes

## Chapter 1

1. Quoted in the *Vancouver Sun* April 21, 2009.
2. Quoted in Debates of the 39th Parliament, 1st session June 13, 2006 at 141.
3. Physical assault is divided into several categories. Common assault is the least serious type, involving pushing, slapping, and punching. Assault with a weapon involves the use of a weapon; assault causing bodily harm has occurred when the victim sustains an injury. Aggravated assault results in a victim being wounded, disfigured, or endangered.
4. In 2009 the Canadian Centre for Justice Statistics changed the way it counted one "case." They adjusted the counts for data since 2002 but did not go back further. This means that we cannot compare counts from previous years with those in the most recent reports.
5. CANSIM Table 2510004 Adult Correctional Services Average Count of Offenders in Provincial, Territorial, Federal Programs Annually (Statistics Canada).
6. For updates on these bills see the information on LEGISinfo, a website that follows government bills through the parliamentary process. The website is available at http://www.parl.gc.ca/LegisInfo.

## Chapter 2

1. Canada has quite a different history than the US, which seems to swing back and forth between competing goals. For example, in the early to mid-twentieth century, many American states favoured rehabilitation to the point of incarcerating offenders until they were "cured." Toward the end of the century, the pendulum had swung the other way, to a model of retributive justice, an approach that will be discussed in the next section of this chapter.

## Chapter 3

1. More information on the panel is available on the web page for Public Safety Canada at http://www.publicsafety.gc.ca/csc-scc/index-eng.aspx.
2. There is no research that assesses the cause of the provincial variability but it may relate to different sentencing patterns or crime rates.
3. Indeterminate sentences are given to offenders who have received the "dangerous offender" designation—only 2 percent of the federal inmate population, approximately four hundred offenders, are serving such a sentence.
4. In recent years we have seen the number of people serving time in provincial remand come close to the number of inmates held in federal institutions.
5. This case is available on the Supreme Court of Canada website at http://www.scc-csc.gc.ca/decisions/index-eng.asp.
6. *The fifth estate* has produced a documentary about Ashley Smith. It can be viewed online at http://www.cbc.ca/fifth/2010-2011/behindthewall. The New Brunswick

Ombudsman also wrote a report that is available at http://www.gnb.ca/0073/PDF/AshleySmith-e.pdf.

7. These statistics were made available through a request made under the Access to Information Act. CSS does not routinely release data on guards' use of force.

8. For more details see *The Economist* article "Rough Justice in America: Too Many Laws, Too Many Prisoners" from July 22, 2010. The article is available online at http://www.economist.com/node/16636027.

## Chapter 4

1. Section 732.1(3)(h) and Section 742.4(2)(f). For more information see Roberts 2004, 69–70. It may be important to distinguish both probation and conditional sentences from suspended sentences. In a suspended sentence the judge holds off on sentencing the offender for a particular period of time. If the offender does not breach conditions or reoffend for the term of the suspension, no sentence is issued. A suspended sentence is therefore indeterminate—the offender does not know the consequence of a breach—and aimed at very low-risk offenders who have committed the least serious crimes. They are essentially warnings rather than punishments (Roberts 2005, 5).

2. R. v. Proulx [2000] 1 S.C.R. 61.

3. Judges can order that an offender serve one half of the sentence before being eligible for parole for some offences, including terrorism and serious drug offences.

## Chapter 5

1. In 1997, for example, the legislation controlling drugs was expanded to include a wider range of substances (Dauvergne 2009).

2. The Canadian Association of Drug Treatment Courts has a web page: http://www.cadtc.org. The United Nations Office on Drugs and Crime has information on its web page at http://www.unodc.org.

3. See http://www.mentalhealthcourt.ca.

4. In a random control, trial participants in drug court are chosen randomly from a list of people who are otherwise eligible to participate.

## Chapter 6

1. More information on the NCPC and the National Crime Prevention Strategy is available at http://www.publicsafety.gc.ca.

2. Public Safety Canada, National Crime Prevention Centre, http://www.publicsafety.gc.ca/prg/cp/index-eng.aspx.

3. The NCPC publications are available on its website at http://www.publicsafety.gc.ca.

4. For more information, see http://www.nationalantidrugstrategy.gc.ca.

5. For details on the CSC policy, see the article "Harm Reduction" by Mary Beth Pongrac in *Focus on Infectious Diseases, CSC Infectious Diseases Newsletter* winter 2006, 4(2) available online at http://www.csc-scc.gc.ca.

6. The list of agencies includes, but is not limited to, the World Health Organization, the Correctional Investigator of Canada, the Canadian Medical Association, the On-

tario Medical Association, the Canadian Human Rights Commission on AIDS and prisons, and the Canadian Association of Mental Health.

7. Summaries of the many research projects related to Insite are provided in a report by the British Columba Centre for Excellence in HIV/AIDS that is available at http://www.uhri.cfenet.ubc.ca.

## Chapter 7

1. The Centre for Restorative Justice at Simon Fraser University has more about his story, and the experiences of others, on its website: http://www.sfu.ca/crj.
2. R. v. Gladue [1999], 171 D.L.R. (4th); R. v. Proulx [2000] SCC 5, [2000] 1 S.C.R. 61.
3. For more information, see "Restorative Justice: Canadian Inventory of Restorative Justice Programs" on the Correction Service of Canada website at http://www.csc-scc.gc.ca/text/rj/crg-eng.shtml.
4. The Nova Scotia program currently deals only with youth between 12 and 17 years old, with nine restorative justice agencies spread across the province (Archibald and Llewellyn 2006). The province is running pilot projects with adults in two regions.

## Conclusion

1. Prior to the passing of this bill, a multiple murderer would have received a parole eligibility period for each murder, but these periods ran concurrently so that they would not have to wait for more than 25 years to be eligible to apply for parole. A multiple murderer may not be eligible for parole for 50 years or more.
2. The faint hope clause applied to offenders who had been sentenced to life with a parole eligibility period of more than 15 years. Offenders were required first to make an application to a judge; the application then required the support of a jury before it could be brought before the parole board.
3. For full details on spending in CSC see a blog by Justin Piché at http://tpcp-canada.blogspot.com. Piché, a sociologist at Memorial University, has spent years compiling data on money being spent on prisons in Canada.
4. The new strategy replaced the older National Drug Strategy. The name change was deliberate. As Tony Clement stated upon announcing the Anti-Drug Strategy: "The party's over for illicit drug users." He was quoted by CBC News, September 27, 2007. See http://www.cbc.ca/news/canada/story/2007/09/29/drug-strategy.html.
5. The Tackling Violent Crime Act also provided for mandatory minimum sentences of three years for some crimes involving a firearm and five years for others. These provisions came into effect in May 2008. According to court data, the mandatory minimum is less time than the typical sentence that has been given out by our courts. For example, in 2005–6, the average sentence for a firearm-related offence was more than four years in prison (Dauvergne and De Socio 2008; Geddes 2009).
6. The document is available at http://www.conservative.ca/policy/platform_2011.
7. In a column in the *Toronto Sun*, Lorrie Goldstein points out that "the violent crime rate in Canada today (meaning 2008, the latest available figures) is 321% above what it was in 1962. ... In 1962 there were 221 violent crimes reported to police per 100,000 people while today [i.e., 2008] the comparable figure is 932 per 100,000, more than a tripling in fewer than 50 years" (Goldstein 2009).
8. For information about this organization see http://crcvc.ca.

# Further Reading

## Chapter 1

Brennan, Shannon, and Mia Dauvergne. 2011. "Police-Reported Crime Statistics in Canada, 2010." *Juristat*. Statistics Canada Catalogue no. 85-002-X. Available online.

Perreault, Samuel, and Shannon Brennan. 2010. "Criminal Victimization in Canada, 2009." *Juristat* 30(2). Statistics Canada Catalogue no. 85-002-X201000211340. Available online.

Piché, Justin. 2010. *Tracking the Politics of "Crime" and Punishment in Canada* (blog). http://tpcp-canada.blogspot.com.

Roberts, Julian, Nicole Crutcher, and Paul Verbrugge. 2007. "Public Attitudes to Sentencing in Canada: Exploring Recent Findings." *Canadian Journal of Criminology and Criminal Justice* 49:75–107.

Roberts, Julian, and Michelle G. Grossman. 2008. *Criminal Justice in Canada: A Reader*. Toronto: Nelson Education.

## Chapter 2

Cayley, David. 1998. *The Expanding Prison: The Crisis in Crime and Punishment and the Search for Alternatives*. Toronto: Anansi.

Doob, Anthony N., and Cheryl Webster. 2003. "Sentence Severity and Crime: Accepting the Null Hypothesis." *Crime and Justice* 30:143–95.

Law Commission of Canada. 2003. "What Is a Crime? Challenges and Alternatives." Ottawa: Law Commission of Canada. Available online.

## Chapter 3

Correctional Investigator of Canada. 2009. "Annual Report of the Office of the Correctional Investigator 2008–2009." Ottawa: Ministry of Public Safety. Available online.

*The Economist*. 2010. "Rough Justice in America: Too Many Laws, Too Many Prisoners." July 22. Available online.

Jackson, Michael. 2002. *Justice Behind the Walls*. Vancouver: Douglas and McIntyre.

*The Journal of Prisoners on Prisons*. Available online at: http://www.jpp.org.

## Chapter 4

Calverley, Donna. 2010. "Adult Correctional Services in Canada 2008/2009." *Juristat* 30(3). Statistics Canada Catalogue no. 85-002-X. Available online.

Correctional Service Canada. 2008. "Protecting Society through Community Corrections." Ottawa: Correctional Service of Canada. Available online.

Roberts, Julian. 2004. *The Virtual Prison: Community Custody and the Evolution of Imprisonment*. Cambridge: Cambridge University Press.

## Chapter 5

Public Safety Canada. 2008. "Toronto Drug Treatment Court Project." Ottawa: Public Safety Canada.

——. 2009. "Drug Treatment Court of Vancouver (DTCV)." Vol. 2010. Ottawa: Public Safety Canada.

Schneider, Richard D., Hy Bloom, and Mark Heerema. 2007. *Mental Health Courts: Decriminalizing the Mentally Ill*. Toronto: Irwin Law.

Ursel, Jane, Leslie Tutty, and Janice LeMaistre, eds. 2008. *What's Law Got to Do With It? The Law, Specialized Courts and Domestic Violence*. Toronto: Cormorant Books Inc.

## Chapter 6

Boyd, Susan, Donald MacPherson, and Bud Osborn. 2009. *Raise Shit! Social Action Saving Lives*. Halifax: Fernwood.

National Crime Prevention Centre. Website available at: http://www.publicsafety.gc.ca.

Schneider, Stephen. 2009. *Crime Prevention: Theory and Practice*. Toronto: CRC Press.

## Chapter 7

The Centre for Restorative Justice. Webiste available at: http://www.sfu.ca/crj.

Nova Scotia Restorative Jusitce-Community University Research Alliance. Website available at: http://www.nsrj-cura.ca.

Woolford, Andrew. 2009. *The Politics of Restorative Justice: A Critical Introduction*. Black Point, NS: Fernwood Publishing.

Zehr, Howard. 1990. *Changing Lenses: A New Focus for Crime and Justice*. Scotdale, PA: Herald Press.

——. 2002. *The Little Book of Restorative Justice*. Intercourse, PA: Good Books.

# References

Adam, Betty Anne. 2009. "Tears Flow at Pauchay's Sentencing Circle." *National Post*, February 13.

Adams, Michael. 1990. "Canadian Attitudes Toward Crime and Justice." Forum on Corrections Research 2.

Adlaf, Edward M., Patricia Begin, and Edward Sawka. 2005. "Canadian Addiction Survey (CAS): A National Survey of Canadians' Use of Alcohol and Other Drugs: Prevalence of Use and Related Harms." Ottawa: Canadian Centre on Substance Abuse.

Alschuler, Albert. 2003. "The Changing Purposes of Criminal Punishment: A Retrospective on the Past Century and Some Thoughts about the Next." *The University of Chicago Law Review* 70.

Anderson, John F. 2001. "What to Do about 'Much Ado' about Drug Courts." *International Journal of Drug Policy* 12:469–75.

Andrews, Duane A., and James Bonta. 2006. *The Psychology of Criminal Conduct*. Newark, NJ: Lexis Nexis.

Angus Reid. 2009a. "Canadians Clearly Support Ideas to Deal with Gang Violence." Angus Reid Strategies. Available online.

———. 2009b. "Canadians Endorse Federal Government's Anti-Crime Proposals." Angus Reid Strategies. Available online.

Archibald, Bruce, and Jennifer Llewellyn. 2006. "The Challenges of Institutionalizing Comprehensive Restorative Justice: Theory and Practice in Nova Scotia." *Dalhousie Law Journal* 29:297.

Aucoin, Kathy, and Diane Beauchamp. 2007. "Impacts and Consequences of Victimization, 2004." *Juristat* 27(1). Statistics Canada Catalogue no. 85-002-X20070019575. Available online.

Austin, James, James Clark, Patricia Hardyman, and Henry Alan. 1999. "The Impact of Three Strikes and You're Out." *Punishment & Society* 1:131–62.

Babooram, Avani. 2008. "The Changing Profile of Adults in Custody, 2006/2007." *Juristat* 28(10). Statistics Canada Catalogue no. 85022X. Available online.

Barnes, The Hon. Mr. Justice Kofi. 2009. "Drug Treatment Courts—Basic Principles." Presented at the Canadian Criminal Justice Association Congress, Halifax, NS.

Beattie, Sara. 2009. "Homicide in Canada, 2008." *Juristat* 29(4). Statistics Canada Catalogue no. 85-002X. Available online.

Belenko, Steven. 1998. "Research on Drug Courts: A Critical Review." *National Drug Court Institute Review* 1:10–55.

Bennet, Guy. 1998. "Safe-Injection Sites Don't Make Sense." *The West End Times*, September 24.

Berman, Greg, and John Feinblatt. 2001. "Problem Solving Courts: A Brief Primer." New York: Center for Court Innovation.

Besserer, Sandra, and Catherin Trainor. 2000. "Criminal victimization in Canada, 1999" *Juristat* 20(10). Statistics Canada Catalogue no. 85-002-XIE. Available online.

Bland, Roger, Stephen Newman, Ronald Dyck, and Helene Orn. 1990. "Prevalence of Psychiatric Disorders and Suicide Attempts in a Prison Population." *Canadian Journal of Psychiatry* 35.

Blomquist, T. 2004. "Restorative Justice—Reflections on Dialogue, Restorative Justice

Kit 2004." Ottawa: Correctional Service Canada.

Bognar, Carl J., Jeanne Legare, and Susan Ross. 1998. "Injection Drug Use and the Epidemic of HIV in the Lower Mainland." Lower Mainland Working Group on Communicable Diseases. Available online.

Bonta, James, Mia Dauvergne, and Tanya Rugge. 2003. "The Reconviction Rate of Federal Offenders 2003–02." Public Safety Canada. Available online.

Bonta, James, Rebecca Jesseman, Tanya Rugge, and Robert Cormier. 2008. "Restorative Justice and Recidivism: Promises Made, Promises Kept?" In *Handbook of Restorative Justice: A Global Perspective*, edited by Dennis Sullivan and Larry Tifft, 108–20. New York: Routledge.

Boyd, Susan, Donald MacPherson, and Bud Osborn. 2009. *Raise Shit! Social Action Saving Lives*. Halifax: Fernwood.

Brien, Al H. 2004. "Mental Health Court . . . Three Years and Counting." *Provincial Judges' Journal* 27:50.

Brochu, Serge, Marie Marthe Cousineau, Michaël Gillet, Louis-Georges Corurnoyer, Kai Pernanen, and Larry Motiuk. 2002. "Drugs, Alcohol, and Criminal Behaviour: A Profile of Inmates in Canadian Federal Institutions." *Forum on Corrections Research* 13(3):20–24.

Bushie, J. 1997. "CHCH Reflections." Ottawa: Ministry of the Solicitor General of Canada.

Cahill, Dan. 1998. "Victimization." *Journal of Prisoners on Prison* 9(2):1–2.

Calverley, Donna. 2010. "Adult Correctional Services in Canada 2008/2009." *Juristat* 30(3). Statistics Canada Catalogue no. 85-002-X. Available online.

Canada. 2011. "The Next Phase of Canada's Economic Action Plan: A Low-Tax Plan for Jobs and Growth Tabled in the House of Commons by the Honourable James M. Flaherty, Minister of Finance." Ottawa: Government of Canada. Available online.

Canadian Centre for Justice Statistics. 2001. "Crime Comparisons between Canada and the United States." *Juristat* 21(11). Statistics Canada Catalogue no. 85-002-X20010118397. Available online.

———. 2008. "Adult Criminal Court Survey 2006/2007." *Juristat* 28(5). Statistics Canada Catalogue no. 85-002-XIE. Available online.

Canadian Council on Social Development. n.d. "Children and Youth Crime Prevention through Social Development." http://www.ccsd.ca/cpsd/ccsd.

Canadian Criminal Justice Association. n.d. "Mandatory Minimum Sentences." Available online.

Canadian Institute for the Administration of Justice. 1997. "Dawn or Dusk: New Beginning or More of the Same." Paper presented at the Dawn or Dusk in Sentencing Conference, Montreal. Available online.

Canadian Press. 2007. "PM Wants Mandatory Sentences for 'Serious' Drug Crimes: Harper Vows to Help Addicts but Punish Traffickers." *CBC News.ca*, October 4.

Cayley, David. 1998. *The Expanding Prison: The Crisis in Crime and Punishment and the Search for Alternatives*. Toronto: Anansi.

Centre for Addiction and Mental Health. n.d. http://www.camh.net.

———. 2002. "CAMH and Harm Reduction: A Background Paper on Its Meaning and Applications for Substance Use Issues." Centre for Addiction and Mental Health. Available online.

Champion, Dean John. 2007. "The History of Crime Prevention in the United States." In *Crime Prevention in America*, edited by Dean J. Campion, 3–28. Upper Saddle River, NJ: Pearson Education.

Chu, Sandra Ka Hon, and Richard Elliott. 2009. "Clean Switch: The Case for Prison

Needle and Syringe Programs." Toronto: Canadian HIV/AIDS Legal Network. Available online.

Chu, Sandra Ka Hon, and Katrina Peddle. 2010. "Under the Skin: A People's Case for Prison Needle and Syringe Programs." Toronto: Canadian HIV/AIDS Legal Network. Available online.

The Church Council on Justice and Corrections. 2008. "Circles of Support and Accountability." Available online.

City of Vancouver. 2008. "Four Pillars Drug Strategy." http://vancouver.ca/fourpillars.

Commissioner of the Correctional Service of Canada. 2009. "Commissioner's Directive 821: Management of Infectious Diseases." Ottawa: Correctional Service of Canada. Available online.

Conservative Party of Canada. 2011. "Here for Canada: Stephen Harpers' Low-Tax Plan for Jobs and Economic Growth." Available online.

Cooley, Dennis. 1993. "Criminal Victimization in Male Federal Prisons." *Canadian Journal of Criminology* 35(4) 479–95.

———. 2002. "Restorative Justice in Canada: Lessons Learned." Ottawa: Law Commission of Canada.

Correctional Investigator. 2006. "Annual Report of the Office of the Correctional Investigator 2005–2006." Gatineau: Minister of Public Works and Government Services Canada. Available online.

———. 2008a. "A Failure to Respond: Correctional Investigator of Canada Releases Report on the Death of a Federal Inmate." Gatineau: Minister of Public Works and Government Services Canada. Available online.

———. 2008b. "A Preventable Death." Gatineau: Minister of Public Works and Government Services Canada. Available online.

———. 2009. "Annual Report of the Office of the Correctional Investigator 2008–2009." Ottawa: Ministry of Public Safety. Available online.

———. 2010. "Annual Report of the Office of the Correctional Investigator 2009–2010." Ottawa: Ministry of Public Safety. Available online.

Correctional Service of Canada. n.d. "Assessing Offender Substance-Abuse Problems at Reception: Preliminary Findings from the Computerized Lifestyle Assessment Instrument." Ottawa: Correctional Service of Canada. Available online.

———. 2009a. "Departmental Performance Report, 2008–2009." Ottawa: Correctional Service of Canada. Available online.

———. 2009b. "Strategic Plan for Aboriginal Corrections: Innovation, Learning & Adjustment 2006–07 to 2010–11." Ottawa: Correctional Service of Canada. Available online.

———. 2010a. "2010–2011 Report on Plans and Priorities." Ottawa: Correctional Service of Canada.

———. 2010b. "Security Incidents with Reported Physical Injuries to Inmates: Fiscal Year 2009–2010." Ottawa: Correctional Service of Canada.

———. 2010c. "Toews: A Safe and Secure Society Is Worth the Cost." News release, November 29. Available online.

———. 2010d. "Use of Force Annual Report: 2009–2010." Ottawa: Correctional Service of Canada.

———. 2011. "2011–2012 Report on Plans and Priorities." Ottawa: Correctional Service of Canada.

Correctional Service of Canada Review Panel. 2007. "Report of the Correctional Service of Canada Review Panel: A Roadmap to Strengthening Public Safety." Gatineau: Minister of Public Works and Government Services Canada. Available online.

Cosden, Merith, Jeffrey K. Ellens, Jeffrey L. Schnell, Yasmeen Yamini-Diouf, and Maren M. Wolfe. 2003. "Evaluation of a Mental Health Treatment Court with Assertive Community Treatment." *Behavioral Sciences & the Law* 21:415–27.

CTV. 2010. "Justice Minister Defends Day's Unreported Crimes Claim." *CTV.ca*, August 4. Available online.

CTV Ottawa. 2010. "Day Says New Prisons Needed for 'Unreported Crimes.'" *CTV.ca*, August 3. Available online.

Daly, K. 2000. "Revisiting the Relationship between Retributive and Restorative Justice." In *Restorative Justice: Philosophy to Practice*, edited by Heather Strang and John Braithwaite, 33–54. Aldershot: Ashgate Publishing.

Dauvergne, Mia. 2009. "Trends in Police-Reported Drug Offences in Canada." *Juristat* 29(2). Statistics Canada Catalogue no. 85-002-X. Available online.

Dauvergne, Mia, and Leonardo De Socio. 2008. "Firearms and Violence Crime." *Juristat* 28(2). Statistics Canada Catalogue no. 85-002-XIE. Available online.

Dauvergne, Mia, and John Turner. 2010. "Police-Reported Crime Statistics in Canada, 2009." *Juristat* 30(2). Statistics Canada Catalogue no. 85-002-X201000211292. Available online.

Davies, Don. 2009. "Debates of the House of Commons." Hansard #96 of the 40th Parliament, 2nd Session. Available online.

Dawson, Myrna, and Ronit Dinovitzer. 2008. "Specialized Justice: From Prosecution to Sentencing in a Toronto Domestic Violence Court." In *What's Law Got To Do With It? The Law, Specialized Courts and Domestic Violence in Canada*, edited by Jane Ursel, Leslie M. Tutty, and Janice LeMaistre, 120–149. Toronto: Cormorant Books Inc.

Doob, Anthony N. 2000. "Transforming the Punishment Environment: Understanding Public Views of What Should Be Accomplished at Sentencing." *Canadian Journal of Criminology* 42:323–40.

Doob, Anthony N., and Julian Roberts. 1983. "An Analysis of the Views of Sentencing." Department of Justice Canada.

Doob, Anthony N., and Cheryl Webster. 2003. "Sentence Severity and Crime: Accepting the Null Hypothesis." *Crime and Justice* 30:143–95.

Dunphy, C. 2007. "'A Monster' No More." *Toronto Star*, September 14. Available online.

Eley, Susan. 2005. "Changing Practices: The Specialised Domestic Violence Court Process." *The Howard Journal of Criminal Justice* 44:113–24.

Farrington, David, and Darryl Davies. 2007. "Repeated Contacts with the Criminal Justice System and Offender Outcomes." Unpublished Report, Canadian Centre for Justice Statistics.

Fish, Morris J. 2008. "An Eye for an Eye: Proportionality as a Moral Principle of Punishment." *Oxford Journal of Legal Studies* 28:51–71.

Gabor, Thomas. 1994. *Everybody Does It: Crime by the Public*. Toronto: University of Toronto Press.

Gaes, Gerald, and Scott Camp. 2009. "Unintended Consequences: Experimental Evidence for the Criminogenic Effect of Prison Security Level Placement on Post-Release Recidivism." *Journal of Experimental Criminology* 5(13): 139–62.

Galloway, Gloria. 2011. "Ottawa Rejects Provincial Bid to Send More Inmates to Federal Prisons." *Globe and Mail*, February 16.

Gannon, Maire. 2004. "General Social Survey on Victimization, Cycle 18: An Overview of Findings." Statistics Canada Catalogue no. 85-568-X.

Gannon, Maire, and Karen Mihorean. 2005. "Criminal Victimization in Canada, 2004."

*Juristat* 25(7). Statistics Canada Catalogue no. 85-002-X20050078803. Available online.

Gannon, Marie, Karen Mihorean, Karen Beattie, Andrea Taylor-Butts, and Rebecca Kong. 2005. "Criminal Justice Indicators." Statistics Canada Catalogue no. 85-227XIE.

Gayle. 2008. "A Life Prisoners' Story." In *Criminal Justice in Canada*, edited by Julian Roberts and Michelle Grossman, 101–11. Toronto: Nelson.

Geddes, John. 2009. "Are We Really Soft on Crime? The Tories Prefer Tough Talk to Hard Proof on Punishment." *Macleans.ca*, November 9. Available online.

Gendreau, Paul, Claire Goggin, and Francis T. Cullen. 1999. "The Effects of Prison Sentences on Recidivism." Ottawa: Solicitor General Canada.

Gendreau, Paul, Claire Goggin, Francis T. Cullen, and Donald Andrews. 1999. "The Effects of Community Sanctions and Incarceration on Recidivism." *Forum on Corrections Research* 12(2): 10–13.

Goldstein, Lorrie. 2009. "'Hug-a-Thug' Crowd Should Read Stats." *Toronto Sun*, October 22. Available online.

Gottfredson, Denise C., and M. Lyn Exum. 2002. "The Baltimore City Drug Treatment Court: One-Year Results from a Randomized Study." *Journal of Research in Crime & Delinquency* 39:337–56.

Greenwood, Peter W. 1998. "Investing in Prisons or Prevention: The State Policy Makers' Dilemma." *Crime & Delinquency* 44:136–42.

Griffiths, Curt, Yvon Dandurand, and Danielle Murdoch. 2007. "The Social Reintegration of Offenders and Crime Prevention." Research Report 2007–2. Ottawa: Public Safety Canada. Available online.

Haggerty, Kevin. 2008. Review of *Evidence-Based Crime Prevention*, by Lawrence W. Sherman, David P. Farrington, Brandon C. Welsh, and Doris Layton Mackenzie, eds. *Theoretical Criminology* 12:116–21.

Hannah-Moffat, Kelly. 2005. "Criminogenic Needs and the Transformative Subject: Hydridisations of Risk/Need in Penality." *Punishment & Society* 7:29–51.

Harper, Stephen. 2010. An address by Stephen Harper, the Prime Minster of Canada, January 25, 2008. Available at http://www.nationalpost.com.

Hathaway, Andrew D., and Kirk I. Tousaw. 2008. "Harm Reduction Headway and Continuing Resistance: Insights from Safe Injection in the City of Vancouver." *International Journal of Drug Policy* 19(1):11–16.

Health Canada. 2002. "A Report on Mental Illness in Canada." Ottawa: Health Canada.

Hoffart, Irene, and Michelle Clarke. 2004. "HomeFront Evaluation Final Report." Calgary: HomeFront Evaluation Committee.

Hoffman, Morris B. 2001. "The Drug Court Scandal." *North Carolina Law Review* 78:1437–534.

Hornick, Joseph P., Michael Boyes, Leslie M. Tutty, and Leah White. 2008. "The Yukon's Domestic Violence Treatment Option: An Evaluation." In *What's Law Got to Do With It? The Law, Specialized Courts and Domestic Violence*, edited by Jane Ursel, Leslie M. Tutty, and Janice LeMaistre, 152–71. Toronto: Cormorant Books.

Hudson, Barbara. 2003. *Understanding Justice: An Introduction to Ideas, Perspectives and Controversies in Modern Penal Theory*. Buckingham, UK: Open University Press.

Hughes, Gordon. 1998. *Understanding Crime Prevention: Social Control, Risk and Late Modernity*. Buckingham, UK: Open University Press.

Hutchinson, Katy. 2010. "Katy Hutchison & Ryan Aldridge (Canada)." The Forgiveness Project. Available online.

International Centre for the Prevention of Crime. 2010. "Crime Prevention and Commu-

nity Safety: Trends and Perspectives." Montreal: International Centre for the Prevention of Crime. Available online.

International Centre for Prison Studies. 2010. "World Prison Brief." London: International Centre for Prison Studies. Available online.

Jackson, Michael, and Graham Stewart. 2009. "A Flawed Compass: A Human Rights
Analysis of the Roadmap to Strengthening Public Safety." *Justice Behind Walls*. Available online.

Jacobs, Mindelle. 2008. "Law's Gone to Pot." *Toronto Sun*. November 14.

Jenkinson, Mike. 2005. "House Arrest Like a Vacation." *Edmonton Sun*, March 14.

John Howard Society of Alberta. 1999. "Sentencing in Canada." http://www
.johnhoward.ab.ca/pub/pdf/C33.pdf.

John Howard Society of Ontario. n.d. "Perspectives on Corrections." http://www.john-
howard.on.ca/pdfs/perspectives_on_correction.pdf.

Johnson, Holly. 2010. "Protecting Victims' Interest in Domestic Violence Court." In *En-
gaging our Communities: Working Together to End Intimate Partner Violence*. University
of New Brunswick: Murial McQueen Fergusson Centre for Family Violence Research.

Johnson, Sara. 2003. "Custodial Remand in Canada." *Juristat* 23(7). Statistics Canada
Catalogue no. 85-002-X20030078420. Available online.

———. 2006. "Outcomes of Probation and Conditional Sentence Supervision: An Analysis of Newfoundland and Labrador, Nova Scotia, New Brunswick, Saskatchewan and
Alberta, 2003/2004 to 2004/2005." *Juristat* 26(7). Statistics Canada Catalogue no.
85-002-XIE. Available online.

Jones, Craig. 2009. "Committee Transcripts: Select Committee on Mental Health and
Addictions." Committee on Mental Health and Addictions, Mental Health and Addictions Strategy. Legislative Assembly of Ontario. Available online.

Kelly, Russ. n.d. "Stories of Reconciliation." Simon Fraser University: Centre for Restorative Justice. Available online.

Kerr, Thomas, Jo-Anne Stoltz, Mark Tyndall, Kathy Li, Ruth Zhang, Julio Montaner,
and Evan Wood. 2006. "Impact of a Medically Supervised Safer Injection Facility
on Community Drug Use Patterns: A Before and After Study." *British Medical Journal*
332(7535):220–22.

Kerr, Thomas, Mark Tyndall, Kathy Li, Julio Montaner, and Evan Wood. 2005. "Safer Injection Facility Use and Syringe Sharing in Injection Drug Users." *Lancet*
366(9482):316–18.

Kerr, Thomas, Mark Tyndall, Ruth Zhang, Calvin Lai, Julio S. G. Montaner, and Evan
Wood. 2007. "Circumstances of First Injection among Illicit Drug Users Accessing
a Medically Supervised Safer Injection Facility." *American Journal of Public Health*
97(7):1228–30.

Kerr, Thomas, Evan Wood, Glenn Betteridge, Rick Lines, and Ralf Jürgens. 2004. "Harm
Reduction in Prisons: A 'Rights Based Analysis.'" *Critical Public Health* 14(4):345–60.

Landry, Laura, and Maire Sinha. 2008. "Adult Correctional Services in Canada,
2005/2006." *Juristat* 28(6). Statistics Canada Catalogue no. 85-002-X200800610593.
Available online.

La Prairie, Carol, Louis Gliksman, Patricia G. Erickson, Ronald Wall, and Brenda New-
ton-Taylor. 2002. "Drug Treatment Courts—A Viable Option for Canada? Sentencing
Issues and Preliminary Findings from the Toronto Court." *Substance Use & Misuse*
37:1529–66.

Latimer, Jeff, and Norm Desjardins. 2007. "The 2007 National Justice Survey: Tackling
Crime and Public Confidence." Ottawa: Department of Justice Canada.

Latimer, Jeff, Craig Dowden, and Danielle Muise. 2005. "The Effectiveness of Restorative Justice Practices: A Meta-analysis." *The Prison Journal* 85(2):127–44. Available online.

Latimer, Jeff, Kelly Morton-Bourgon, and Jo-Anne Crétien. 2006. "A Meta-Analytic Examination of Drug Treatment Courts: Do They Reduce Recidivism?" Ottawa: Department of Justice Canada.

Law Commission of Canada. 2003. "What Is a Crime? Challenges and Alternatives." Ottawa: Law Commission of Canada. Available online.

Lind, Bronwyn, Don Weatherburn, Shuling Chen, Marian Shanahan, Emily Lancsar, and Marion Haas. 2002. "New South Wales Drug Court Evaluation Cost-Effectiveness." Sydney, Australia: New South Wales Bureau of Criminal Statistics and Research.

Llewellyn, Jennifer, and Robert Howse. 1999. "Restorative Justice—A Conceptual Framework." Ottawa: Law Commission of Canada.

MADD Canada. 2004. "Over 33,000 Petitioners Urge End to Conditional Sentences." News release, November 16. Available online.

Maidment, Madonna R. 2002. "Toward a 'Woman-Centred' Approach to Community-Based Corrections: A Gendered Analysis of Electronic Monitoring (EM) in Eastern Canada." *Women and Criminal Justice* 13: 47–68.

Makin, Kirk. 2010. "Canadians' Views on Crime Are Hardening, Poll Finds." *Globe and Mail*, January 21.

Marshall, Brandon D.L., M.J. Milloy, Evan Wood, Julio S.G. Montaner, and Thomas Kerr. 2011. "Reduction in Overdose Mortality after the Opening of North America's First Medically Supervised Safer Injecting Facility: A Retrospective Population-Based Study." *Lancet* 377(9775):1429–37.

Marshall, Tony F. 1999. "Restorative Justice: An Overview." London: Home Office, Research Development and Statistics Directorate.

Marth, Michael. 2008. "Adult Criminal Court Statistics, 2006/2007." *Juristat* 28(5). Statistics Canada Catalogue no. 85-002-X200800510567. Available online.

Martinson, Robert. 1974. "What Works? Questions and Answers about Prison Reform." *The Public Interest* 35:22–54.

Marutto, Paula, and Kelly Hannah-Moffat. 2006. "Assembling Risk and the Restructuring of Penal Control." *British Journal of Criminology* 46:438–54.

Mayeda, Andrew. 2009. "Tories Move to Eliminate 'Two-for-One' Jail Time Credit." *National Post*, March 25.

McKie, David. 2011. "Tory Crime Plan Fails Victims, Inmates: Critics." *CBC.ca*, February 16. Available online.

Ministry of Community Safety and Correctional Services. 2008. "A Safe, Strong, Secure Ontario: Strategic Plan 2008–2013." Toronto: Ministry of Community Safety and Correctional Services.

Monture-Angus, P. 1999. *Journeying Forward: Dreaming First Nations' Independence*. Halifax: Fernwood.

Moore, Dawn. 2007. "Review of the Virtual Prison: Community Custody and the Evolution of Imprisonment." *Punishment & Society* 9(3): 9339–341.

———. 2009. "The Drug Treatment Court Movement." *Criminal Justice Matters* 75:30–31.

National Crime Prevention Centre. 2009. "Supporting the Successful Implementation of the National Crime Prevention Strategy." Catalogue no. PS4-74/2009E-PD. Ottawa: National Crime Prevention Centre.

New Brunswick Ombudsman and Child and Youth Advocate. 2008. "The Ashley Smith Report." Ombudsman and Child and Youth Advocate. Available online.

Nicholson, Rob. 2009. "Legislation Introduced to End Conditional Sentences for Serious Property and Violent Crime." News release, June 15. Available online.

Olley, Maureen, Tonia Nicholls, and Johann Brink. 2009. "Mentally Ill Individuals in Limbo: Obstacles and Opportunities for Providing Psychiatric Services to Corrections Inmates with Mental Illness." *Behavioral Sciences and the Law* 27(5):811–31.

Osler, Hugh. 2010. Letter to Vic Toews. April 6. Canadian Criminal Justice Association. *Justice Report* 25(2).

Paciocco, David. 1999. *Getting Away with Murder: The Canadian Criminal Justice System.* Toronto: Irwin Law.

Parole Board of Canada. 2009. "Performance Monitoring Report, 2008–2009." Ottawa: Parole Board of Canada. Available online.

Peachey, Dean. 1989. "The Kitchener Experiment." In *Mediation and Criminal Justice: Victims, Offenders and Community*, edited by Martha Wright and Burt Galaway, 14–26. London: Sage.

Perreault, Samuel, and Shannon Brennan. 2010. "Criminal Victimization in Canada, 2009." *Juristat* 30(2). Statistics Canada Catalogue no. 85-002-X201000211340. Available online.

Petrellis, Tania R. 2007. "The Restorative Justice Living Unit at Grande Cache Institution: Exploring the Application of Restorative Justice in a Correctional Environment." Ottawa: Correctional Service of Canada. Available online.

Piché, Justin. 2010. *Tracking the Politics of "Crime" and Punishment in Canada* (blog). http://tpcp-canada.blogspot.com.

Poulin, Celine, Michel Alary, Gilles Lambert, Gaston Godin, Suzanne Landry, Helene Gagnon, Eric Demers, Elena Morarescu, Jean Rochefort, and Christiane Claessens. 2008. "Prevalence of HIV and Hepatitis C Virus Infections Among Inmates of Quebec Provincial Prison." *Canadian Medical Association Journal* 177(3):252–56.

Poulson, Barton. 2003. "A Third Voice: A Review of Empirical Research on the Psychological Outcomes of Restorative Justice." *Utah Law Review* (1):167–203.

Pranis, Kay. 2010. "Reflecting on the Relationship of the Community and Restorative Justice, Reflexions Past, Present and Future: Restorative Justice Week 2010." Ottawa: Correctional Services of Canada.

Public Health Agency of Canada. 2006. "Prison Needle Exchange: Review of the Evidence." Ottawa: Correctional Service of Canada.

Public Safety Canada. 2007. "Rehabilitation Starts on Day One." Ottawa: Public Safety Canada. Available online.

———. 2008. "Toronto Drug Treatment Court Project." Ottawa: Public Safety Canada.

———. 2009a. "Drug Treatment Court of Vancouver (DTCV)." Vol. 2010. Ottawa: Public Safety Canada.

———. 2009b. "A Day in the Life of an Inmate." Ottawa: Public Safety Canada. Available online.

———. 2010. "Government Takes Action to End Early Release of Criminals and Increase Offender Accountability." News release, June 15. Available online.

Rajekar, Ashutosh, and Ramnarayanan Mathilakath. 2010. "The Funding Requirement and Impact of the 'Truth in Sentencing Act' on the Correctional System in Canada." Ottawa: Office of the Parliamentary Budget Officer.

Richards, Lenore. 2000. "Restorative Justice and the RCMP: Definitions and Directions." *RCMP Gazette* 62(5/6): 8–11.

Roberts, Ann. 2004. "Is Restorative Justice Tied to Specific Models of Practice?" In *Critical Issues in Restorative Justice*, edited by Howard Zehr and Barb Toews, 241–52. Monsey, NY: Criminal Justice Press.

Roberts, Julian. 2001. "Fear of Crime and Attitudes to Criminal Justice in Canada: A Review of Recent Trends 2001–02." Ottawa: Public Safety Canada. Available online.

———.2002. "The Evolution of Conditional Sentencing: An Empirical Analysis." *Criminal Reports* 3(6th series):267–83.

———. 2004a. "Public Confidence in Criminal Justice: A Review of Recent Trends 2004–05." Ottawa: Public Safety Canada. Available online.

———. 2004b. *The Virtual Prison: Community Custody and the Evolution of Imprisonment.* Cambridge: Cambridge University Press.

Roberts, Julian, Nicole Crutcher, and Paul Verbrugge. 2007. "Public Attitudes to Sentencing in Canada: Exploring Recent Findings." *Canadian Journal of Criminology and Criminal Justice* 49:75–107.

Roberts, Julian, and Thomas Gabor. 2004. "Living in the Shadow of Prison: Lessons from the Canadian Experience in Decarceration." *British Journal of Criminology* 44: 92–112.

Robinson, David, and Luisa Mirabelli. 1995. "National Inmate Survey: Final Report." Ottawa: Correctional Service of Canada. Available online.

Rosenthal, Jeffrey. 2005. *Struck by Lightning: The Curious World of Probabilities.* Toronto: Harper Collins.

Sanders, Trevor, and Julian Roberts. 2000. "Public Attitudes toward Conditional Sentencing: Results of a National Survey." *Canadian Journal of Behavioural Science* 32(4):199–207.

Sauvé, Julie, and Kwing Hung. 2008. "An International Perspective on Criminal Victimization." *Juristat* 28(10). Statistics Canada Catalogue no. 85-002-X200801010745. Available online.

Schneider, Richard D., Hy Bloom, and Mark Heerema. 2007. *Mental Health Courts: Decriminalizing the Mentally Ill.* Toronto: Irwin Law.

Schneider, Stephen. 2009. *Crime Prevention: Theory and Practice.* Toronto: CRC Press.

Scott, R. 2000. "Testimony at the Standing Committee on Justice and Human Rights." 36th Parliament 2nd session ed., pp. at 950.

Shaw, Margaret, and Caroline Andrew. 2005. "Engendering Crime Prevention: International Developments and the Canadian Experience." *Canadian Journal of Criminology & Criminal Justice* 47(2):293–316.

Sherman, Lawrence W., David Farrington, Brandon Welsh, and Dorris MacKenzie. 2002. *What Works, What Doesn't, What's Promising and Future Directions.* London: Routledge.

Sherman, Lawrence W., Denise Gottfredson, Doris MacKenzie, John Eck, Peter Reuter, and Shawn Bushway. 1998. "Preventing Crime: What Works, What Doesn't, What's Promising." Washington, DC: National Institute of Justice.

Sherman, Lawrence W., and Heather Strang. 2007. "Restorative Justice: The Evidence." London: The Smith Institute.

Sinclair, The Honourable Justice Murray. 2010. "Truth and Reconciliation Commission of Canada: For the Child Taken, For the Parent Left Behind." Presented at the 9th Session of the United Nations Permanent Forum on Indigenous Issues, United Nations, NY, April 27.

Skolnick, Jerome H. 1995. "What Not to Do About Crime: The American Society of Criminology 1994 Presidential Address." *Criminology* 33.

Slinger, Emily, and Ronald Roesch. 2010. "Problem-Solving Courts in Canada: A Review and a Call for Empirically Based Evaluation Methods." *International Journal of Law & Psychiatry* 33:258–64.

Small, Will, S. Kain, Nancy Laliberte, Martin T. Schechter, Michael V. O'Shaughnessy, and Patricia M. Spittal. 2005. "Incarceration, Addiction and Harm Reduction: Inmates Experience Injecting Drugs in Prison." *Substance Use and Misuse* 40(6):831–43.

Smith, Paula, Claire Goggin, and Paul Gendreau. 2002. "The Effects of Prison Sentences and Intermediate Sanctions on Recidivism: General Effects and Individual Differences 2002–01." Gatineau: Public Works and Government Services Canada.

Statistics Canada. n.d. "Adult Correctional Services, Average Counts of Offenders in Provincial, Territorial and Federal Programs, Annual." CANSIM data, Table 2510004.

———. 2003. "Canadian Community Health Survey: Mental Health and Well-Being." Ottawa: Statistics Canada.

———. 2004. "Canada's Community Health Survey: Mental Health and Well Being." Ottawa: Statistics Canada.

Stein, Karin. 2001. "Public Perception of Crime and Justice in Canada: A Review of Opinion Polls." Ottawa: Department of Justice Canada. Available online.

Stuart, Barry. 1997. "Building Community Partnerships: Community Peacemaking Circles." Ottawa: Department of Justice. Available online.

Stuart, Barry, and Kay Pranis, eds. 2008. *Peacemaking Circles: Reflections and Principal Features and Primary Outcomes*. New York, NY: Routledge.

Sullivan, Steve. 2010. "Was I really a stooge?" in *Crime Victim Advocacy* (blog). http://advocateforvictims.blogspot.com/2010/05/was-i-really-stooge.html.

Taillon, Jaques. 2006. "Offences against the Administration of Justice, 1994/95 to 2003/04." *Juristat* 26(1). Statistics Canada Catalogue no. 85-002-X20060018985. Available online.

Taylor-Butts, Andrea. 2008. "Fact Sheet—Police-Reported Spousal Violence in Canada." In *Family Violence in Canada: A Statistical Profile*, 24–31. Statistics Canada.

Toews, Vic. 2006. "Speech for the Minister of Justice and Attorney General of Canada." Ottawa: Department of Justice. Available online.

———. 2010. "Crime Statistics Fact and Fiction." *VicToews.com*, July 30. Available online.

Tonry, Michael. 2009. "The Mostly Unintended Effects of Mandatory Penalties: Two Centuries of Consistent Findings." *Crime and Justice* 38(1):65–114.

Tufts, Jennifer. 2000. "Public Attitudes toward the Criminal Justice System." *Juristat* 20(12). Statistics Canada Catalogue no. 85-002-X20000128385. Available online.

Tufts, Jennifer, and Julian V. Roberts. 2002. "Sentencing Juvenile Offenders: Comparing Public Preferences and Judicial Practice." *Criminal Justice Policy Review* 13:46–64.

Turner, Susan, Douglas Longshore, Suzanne Wenzel, Elizabeth Deschenes, Peter Greenwood, Terry Fain, Adele Harrell, Andrew Morral, Faye Taxman, Martin Iguchi, Judith Greene, and Duane McBride. 2002. "A Decade of Drug Treatment Court Research." *Substance Use & Misuse* 37(12–13):1489–527.

Tutty, Leslie M., Kevin McNichol, and Janie Christensen. 2008. "Calgary's Home Front Specialized Domestic Violence Court." In *What's Law Got to Do With It? The Law, Specialized Courts and Domestic Violence*, edited by Jane Ursel, Leslie M. Tutty, and Janice LeMaistre. 152–71. Toronto: Cormorant Books.

Tutty, Leslie M., Jane Ursel, and Fiona Douglas. 2008. "Specialized Domestic Violence Courts: A Comparison of Models." In *What's Law Got to Do With It? The Law, Specialized Courts and Domestic Violence*, edited by Jane Ursel, Leslie M. Tutty, and Janice LeMaistre, 69–94. Toronto: Cormorant Books.

Ulmer, Jeffery. 2001. "Intermediate Sanctions: A Comparative Analysis of the Probability and Severity of Recidivism." *Sociological Inquiry* 71(2):164–93.

United Nations. 2002. "Commission for Crime Prevention and Criminal Justice, Report on the 11th session." April.

United Nations Economic and Social Council. 2000. "Basic Principles on the Use of Restorative Justice Programmes in Criminal Matters." United Nations Economic and Social Council.

United Nations Office on Drugs and Crime. 2011. "UNODC and Drug Treatment Courts." United Nations Office on Drugs and Crime. Available online.

Ursel, Jane. 2000. "Winnipeg Family Violence Court Report." In *Family Violence in Canada: A Statistical Profile, 2000*. Ottawa: Centre for Justice Statistics, Statistics Canada.

Ursel, Jane, and Christine Hagyard. 2008. "The Winnipeg Family Violence Court." In *What's Law Got to Do With It? The Law, Specialized Courts and Domestic Violence*, edited by Jane Ursel, Leslie M. Tutty, and Janice LeMaistre, 95–120. Toronto: Cormorant Books.

Valpy, Michael. 2011. "A Pollster's Painful Reckoning: 'How Could I Have Screwed Up So Badly?'" *Globe and Mail*, June 17. Available online.

van Dijk, Jan, John van Kesteren, and Paul Smit. 2007. "Criminal Victimisation in International Perspective: Key Findings from the 2004–2005 ICVS and EUICS." Boom Juridische Uitgevers.

Van Loan, Peter. 2009a. Interviewed by Jan Wong. *The Current*. CBC Radio, September 24.

———. 2009b. "Tory Plans for US Style Prisons Slammed in Report." *Cbc .ca*, September 24. Available online.

von Hirsch, Andrew, Anthony Bottoms, Elizabeth Burney, and P.O. Wikstrom. 1999. *Criminal Deterrence and Sentence Severity: An Analysis of Recent Research*. Oxford: Hart Publishing.

Walgrave, Lode. 2004. "Has Restorative Justice Appropriately Responded to Retribution Theory and Impulses?" In *Critical Issues in Restorative Justice*, edited by Barbara Toews and Howard Zehr. Monsey, NY: Criminal Justice Press.

———. 2005. "Towards Restoration as the Mainstream in Youth Justice." In *New Directions in Restorative Justice: Issues, Practice, Evaluation*, edited by E. Elliot & R. M. Gordon, 3–25. Portland, OR: Willan Publishing.

Wallace, Marnie. 2009. "Police-Reported Crime Statistics in Canada, 2008." *Juristat* 29(3). Statistics Canada Catalogue no. 85-002-X200900310902. Available online.

Wallace, Marnie, John Turner, Anthony Matarazzo, and Colin Babyak. 2009. "Measuring Crime in Canada: Introducing the Crime Severity Index and Improvements to the Uniform Crime Reporting Survey." Statistics Canada Catalogue no. 85-004-X.

Ward, Tony, Joseph Melser, and Pamela M. Yates. 2007. "Reconstructing the Risk-Need-Responsivity Model: A Theoretical Elaboration and Evaluation." *Aggression and Violent Behavior* 12:208–28.

Wattenberg, Ben. 1993. "Crime Solution—Lock 'Em Up." *Wall Street Journal*, December 17.

Weekes, John R., William A. Millson, F.J. Porporino, and D. Robinson. 1994. "The Offender Substance Abuse Pre-Release Program: Intermediate and Post-Release Outcomes." Ottawa: Research and Statistics Branch, Correctional Service of Canada.

Welsh, Brandon C., and David P. Farrington. 2005. "Evidence-Based Crime Prevention." *Canadian Journal of Criminology and Criminal Justice* 47(2):337–54.

Werb, Daniel, and Thomas Kerr. 2007. "Drug Treatment Courts in Canada: An Evidence-Based Review." *HIV/AIDS Policy and Law Review* 12:12–17.

Wherry, Aaron. 2010. "Speaking for the Victims." *Macleans.ca*, September 20. Available online.

White, Vern. 2010. Personal Communication (email), December 23. Halifax.

Wilson, David B., Ojmarrh Mitchell, and Doris L. Mackenzie. 2006. "A Systematic Review of Drug Court Effects on Recidivism." *Journal of Experimental Criminology* 2:459–87.

Wilson, Robin J., Janice E. Picheca, and Michelle Prinzo. 2005. "Circles of Support & Accountability: An Evaluation of the Pilot Project in South-Central Ontario." Ottawa: Correctional Service of Canada.

———. 2007. "Evaluating the Effectiveness of Professionally Facilitated Volunteerism in the Community-Based Management of High-Risk Sexual Offenders: Part One— Effects on Participants and Stakeholders." *The Howard Journal of Criminal Justice* 46(3):289–307.

Woolford, Andrew. 2009. *The Politics of Restorative Justice: A Critical Introduction.* Black Point, NS: Fernwood Publishing.

Zehr, Howard. 1990. *Changing Lenses: A New Focus for Crime and Justice.* Scotdale, PA: Herald Press.

———. 2002. *The Little Book of Restorative Justice.* Intercourse, PA: Good Books.

# Index

# Credits

The publisher is grateful to the following for their permission to reproduce material contained in this book. Every possible effort has been made to trace the original source of quoted material. Where the attempt has been unsuccessful, the publisher would be pleased to hear from copyright holders to rectify any errors or omissions.

"Dawn or Dusk: New Beginning or More of the Same." Originally presented at the CIAJ conference Dawn or Dusk in Sentencing held in Montreal, Quebec, April 1997.

Excerpts from *The Expanding Prison* copyright 1998 David Cayley. Reproduced with permission from House of Anansi Press.

Gayle. 2008. "A Life Prisoners' Story." From ROBERTS. *Criminal Justice in Canada*, 3E. © 2008 Nelson Education Ltd. Reproduced by permission. www.cengage.com/permissions

364
.971
Cro

Crocker, D.
Crime in Canada.
Aurora P.L.  JAN12
33164004640269